The Exceptional Man

Bold, Balanced, and Biblical

M. S. Shiflett

**Pleasant View Baptist Press
pleasantview.org**

Copyright © 2006 by M. S. Shiflett

The Exceptional Man
by M. S. Shiflett

Printed in the United States of America
by Faith Baptist Church Publications
Ft. Pierce, Florida
FBCPublications.com

ISBN 1-60034-740-1

All rights reserved solely by the author. The author guarantees all contents are original and do not infringe upon the legal rights of any other person or work. No part of this book may be reproduced in any form without the permission of the author.

All Scripture references are from the Authorized King James Version of the Bible.

Dedication

This book is dedicated to my lovely wife, Grace Elizabeth and my four precious children, Marissa Grace, Spencer Dean, Stuart Lane and Callie Brooke – my constant motivation to be *The Exceptional Man.*

"For if a man know not how to rule his own house, how shall he take care of the church of God?" **I Timothy 3:5**

Acknowledgments

A special thanks to Yolandi Grové, Deborah South, and Wanda Davidson for their meticulous proofreading.
Your careful reading, critiquing, editing and helpful suggestions are very much appreciated.

Table of Contents

Prologue 11

Chapter One – The Exceptional Man's God 13
- Why Am I Here? 14
- God Builds 15
- God's Men Build 16
- What Are You Building? 17
- Living the Good Life 18

Chapter Two - There's A Famine In the Land 19
- Where are the Men? 20
- David: A Man's Man 25
- Manhood Under Attack 27
- The Death of Manliness 28
- God is Looking for a Man 32

Chapter Three – The Exceptional Man versus the Common Man 37
- The Bold Man 38
- The Balanced Man 41
- The Biblical Man 43
- The Foolish Man 46

Chapter Four – The Exceptional Man's Godliness 49
- Godly Actions 50
- Sexual Purity 52
- A Godly Attitude 53
- Godly Attitude on the Job 54

Chapter Five – The Exceptional Man's Gumption 59
- Boldness of Enterprise 62
- Initiative 64
- Aggressiveness and Guts 65

Chapter Six – The Exceptional Man's Goals 69
- The Plague of Apathy 70
- Taking Control of Your Life 71
- What Are Your Plans? 74
- The Proper Perspective on Riches 76
- Who Are You Trying to Please? 78
- Are You For Real? 79

Chapter Seven – The Exceptional Man's Guidance 83
- Curses and Chores 84
- Who's in Charge? 86
- Character 88
- Convictions 90
- Compassion 93
- Control 95

Chapter Eight – The Exceptional Man's Giving 101
- Selflessness 102
- Should I Tithe? 105
- A Cheerful Giver 107

Chapter Nine – The Exceptional Man's Going 109
- The Great Commission 109
- Spectators and Participators 111
- My Testimony 113

Chapter Ten – The Exceptional Man's Growth 121
- Stale and Stagnant Saints 121
- Growing in Knowledge 122
- Practical Applications 124
- Apollos 127
- Growing in Grace 128

Chapter Eleven – The Exceptional Man's Guarding 133
- You are a Target 134
- Establishing Safeguards 135
- Dating Guidelines 136
- Pornography 137
- Television 139
- Guarding Your Home 140
- The Danger of Daycare 141
- The Public School Fiasco 142
- Conclusion 145

Epilogue – The Exceptional Man's Gospel 147
- Man's Number One Problem 148
- The Proofs of Salvation 150
- Where Are You Going When You Die? ... 152
- Believing Jesus is the Only Way 155
- Repent of Your Sins 156

Prologue

God's crowning creation was Adam – a man that was created in His own image. It is almost impossible to grasp the concept that was God's intention. When He created man, He wanted to produce a living, breathing representation of Himself on Earth. He had countless multitudes of angels surrounding Him, ministering to Him and glorifying Him. He had Heaven and all of its beauty and splendor to enjoy. At some point in ages past, God longed for the worship and adoration of a special creation. A creation that would love Him because they chose to. He created the world in just six days, and on the sixth day, God made man. He formed him from the dust of the ground and breathed into his nostrils the breath of life, and man became a living soul: an eternal, never-dying soul that could never be destroyed.

The first five days of creation were complete and perfect in every way. The trees, the plants, the animals and the landscape were created; and God said at the end of each day that it was good. He was pleased with His creation. Everything looked wonderful. The earth was in perfect, pristine condition; not a flaw or glitch anywhere. On the sixth day He created man, and the Bible tells us in Genesis chapter 1, verse 31, "And

God saw everything that he had made, and behold, it was very good . . . ." Sometime after that, man fell into sin and was expelled from the Garden.

Since that day, man has had to struggle to survive. He has had to labor and toil and sweat. The daily lives of men have been nothing but one struggle on top of another. Financial, emotional, physical, social and spiritual turmoil have taken their toll on mankind. We have come a long way from that perfect man in the Garden of Eden. On that fateful day in a perfect environment when the only man on the planet deliberately violated the direct command of his Maker, things began to change.

From the immediate repercussions of aprons of fig leaves, eviction and curses, our civilization has spiraled into a society plagued with famines, pestilences, wars and every other horror known to mankind. The first man's biggest concern was getting a crop out of the ground. Our concerns involve nuclear war, terrorism and conspiracies on the political front; apostasy and spiritual famine in our churches. The world has changed. Satan is having a field day. Mankind has never been the same. Would God's original plan for man to be a representative of Himself ever come to fruition? Would it ever be possible? What would become of mankind - God's crowning handiwork?

Chapter One

The Exceptional Man's God

We should immediately establish an undeniable fact. *The Exceptional Man* has a God. He has an acute awareness of a Higher Power and is serious about pleasing Him. The God of The Exceptional Man is not a god or a force or an idea that is man-made. This God is the Creator of the Universe and the one, true God; the God of Abraham, Isaac and Jacob; the God of the Bible; Jehovah God.

Having established what may appear on the surface to be an insignificant precedent, we are now faced with understanding the expectations of this Supreme Being: Understanding that he was created by God for a specific purpose now places the entire existence of man in its proper perspective. For a man to deny God is to deny any accountability or reason for living. To deny the Biblical account of Creation is to completely eradicate any and all Divine expectations for that creation. The Evolutionists think that by denying God's existence and God's creation, it alleviates their accountability to Him. They will go to absurd lengths to justify their false theories and rebellion but that will not work. Man's responsibility to serve his purpose for existence is not an option; it is an obligation.

Why Am I Here?

God created the world and He created man. He created the world for a reason, and He created man for a reason. The result of man's failure to understand God's reason for his creation is a man that wanders through life without a purpose. God never did anything without having a Divine plan. God did not create man just for the fun of it. God was not bored and in search of recreation when He fashioned Adam from the dust of the ground. God was not simply testing His Sovereign powers when He breathed into his nostrils the breath of life and man became a living soul. God had a plan for that man. He has a plan for every man. If a man's life is just a chaotic, robotic existence, it is simply because he has not understood God's reason for creating him.

In this book we will come to understand how man can fulfill God's expectations of him. Understanding God's expectations and knowing how to fulfill them will provide us with a clearer picture of what life is all about. Our life is not our own. The time we have been allotted on this earth is the time that God has allowed us to perform the task for which we were created. Many men's first and foremost mistake is thinking that they are their own boss. They think they can do what they want, whenever they want, anytime they want. That is such a perverted viewpoint of one's existence. God did not create you for you to pursue your own interests. God did not give you breath to just sit back and let you do your own thing. The fact that you were born proves that you have a mission in life – to fear God and keep His commandments (Ecclesiastes 12:13).

God Builds

One of the most consistent attributes of God is His constructive nature. God builds. Satan breaks down. God creates. Satan crushes. God constructs. Satan destroys. An excellent example of this fact is seen in the life of Job. God acknowledged that Job was the greatest man in the empire (Job 1:1), the greatest man in the east (Job 1:3), and the greatest man in the earth (Job 1:8). Satan was quick to admit that God was the cause of Job's success. He accused Job of only serving God because of God's blessings and goodness (Job 1:10).

Yet what does Satan do the first chance he gets? In about a thirty minute span of time, he completely destroyed every trace of God's blessings. He destroyed his crops, his caretakers, his commerce and his children. Satan makes life miserable; God makes life worth living. Later on, we find in the last chapter of Job that God rebuilt everything that Satan had torn down. God is a constructive God. God is interested in building and improving what already exists. It is impossible to miss this part of God's character.

Our Bible begins with God building a universe. He takes darkness and formless void and replaces it with light, loveliness and life. His first five days of work were perfect in every way. There was no way He could improve the plants and the animals. Everything was good. Then He created man. Man was also perfect, created in the image of God - a living, breathing representation of God on earth. Of course, this did not set too well with the Destroyer. His immediate reaction was to invalidate God's perfect creation. He first cast doubt on God's explicit instructions. By causing man to second-guess God's plan, he succeeded in causing man to sin. In doing so, man was plunged into a state of sinfulness, shame and suffering. Satan was thrilled. God's construction project was lying in ruins.

God, being a Builder, simply started over. He took the broken, battered remnants and began building once again. By doing so, He revealed His other character traits: love, longsuffering, mercy, compassion and forgiveness. Since the fall of man, God has been working toward fulfilling His original plan – making man a representation of Himself on earth. All throughout the Scripture, every command, every precept and every law that was given was to point man in that direction. To make man a useful tool in the hand of God; to fulfil a specific purpose. In other words, God is building men, so they in turn can also build.

God's Men Build

It is actually amazing when you begin to think of all the great men of the Bible. It is fascinating to discover how many of them were involved in some kind of building project! Noah was given the overwhelming task of building an ark to preserve his family. Abraham went off in search of a city whose Builder and Maker was God. Moses built a Tabernacle in the wilderness. David and Solomon spent years preparing and building a temple for the Lord. Nehemiah and his people rebuilt the walls of Jerusalem. John the Baptist spent six months laying a foundation upon which Christ would build His church. The apostles spent their entire life building on that foundation and adding to the church that Jesus had started. Don't you think it ironic that Jesus spent His first thirty years on earth as a carpenter? God's men are always busy building something.

In I Corinthians chapter three, Paul reminds every one of us that we should be busy building. "According to the grace of God which is given unto me, as a wise masterbuilder, I have laid the foundation, and another buildeth thereon. But let every man take heed how he buildeth thereupon" (vs. 10). Prior to this exhortation, Paul makes a very interesting statement that puts this all in perspective. Paul said in verse 9, "For we are labourers together with God: ye are God's husbandry, ye are God's building."

Get this picture. If you are a born again child of God, you are God's building. He's working on you and building on you to make you more like Christ. In the process, while God is building on you, you are commanded to also build! Jude put it this way in verse 20, "building up yourselves on your most holy faith. . . ." God is building, and you are supposed to be building. It is just that simple.

What Are You Building?

The question is this: What exactly are you building? What are you working on? Is it a savings account? A car? A house? Are you busy building an empire around you for others to covet and desire? Are you building a name for yourself or are you building up the name of Christ? In order to please God, you should be busy furthering His work, His ministry, His purpose – not yours.

> *"I'm not afraid of being a failure. I'm afraid of being successful at something God is not interested in!"*
> - **Dr. Charles Keene**

In order to fulfil the purpose of God, you should be making a constructive contribution to something that God has started. It could be building your children into God-fearing men and women. It could be building your local church into a reckonable force in your community. It could be putting this nation back on track. See, God builds individuals. Individuals build families. Families build churches. Churches build the Body of Christ. If God is building you, but you're not building someone else or something else, you are a selfish, disappointing waste of God's effort. If God is not building you, then you are a selfish, rebellious disappointment to God and His purpose.

Either way, if your life is a failure, it is not God's fault. God never intended for His crowning creation to have to settle for a miserable existence.

Living The Good Life

God loves you. God wants to bless you in ways you never imagined. Jesus put it as clear as He possibly could when He explained, "The thief cometh not, but for to steal, and to kill, and to destroy: I am come that they might have life, and that they might have it more abundantly" (John 10:10). Here Jesus put the facts out in plain view. He said that if something is missing in your life and you feel dead inside, something is bad wrong. If your life and your world are falling apart, it is because the thief, Satan, has had his will and his way in your life. On the other hand, if you allow God to perform His desire, it will result in not only life, but abundant life! Blessings, joy, peace, satisfaction, delight, excitement, strength, and fulfillment will be the results of a surrendered heart and life. Imagine waking up every day with an abundant life staring you in the face!

Can you fathom that? Does it sound too good to be true? Does a life that has meaning and purpose and is worth living sound like a fairy tale to you? Take heart! Take courage! There is hope! God wants to build you and work in your life so you will not be just a man, but an exceptional man – a man that has realized God's plan for his life.

In the following chapters, we will examine God's detailed, definite plan for every man. If you sincerely desire to experience the blessings of God in your life, you must pay close attention to the aspects of a man's life about which God has given clear instruction. In God's sovereignty, He has clearly prescribed the remedy for the common man. It's up to you to take your medicine.

Chapter Two

There's A Famine In The Land

*"And I sought for a man among them,
that should make up the hedge,
and stand in the gap before me for the land,
that I should not destroy it: but I found none."*
(Ezekiel 22:30)

There is a disturbing trend that seems to be escalating at an alarming rate. That trend is the diminishing number of godly, Christian men. Satan has effectively waged an unprecedented onslaught against the Biblical definition of "faithful men". His tactics have not been new; just revised and modernized. The same tricks he used in centuries past to undermine empires, he is using today with an uncanny effectiveness. His deadly and devastating plan is to rid civilization of one of its most powerful stabilizing forces – men of God.

Where Are The Men?

The attack against our pastors, laymen, teachers, deacons, dads and husbands has proven to be a successful attack on Christianity. Satan's cleverly devised schemes have had an incalculable effect on the family, the church and the nation. The death knell began ringing years ago, but we were too deaf to hear it. The clock has been ticking for a long time, marking the gradual but undeniable extinction of a breed of humanity – godly men. What used to be a revered and formidable entity has now become so rare that the next generation is severely lacking proper role models. To whom will our sons look for support and encouragement in their quest for godliness? Where can they go to learn the lifestyle of a faithful, godly man?

My worst fear is that in the near future, the pressure to conform to the world's standards of manhood will be so overwhelming that the next generation will never witness the blessing and the presence of godly men in their world. They will read about it and hear stories about it, but will never experience it for themselves. A lifestyle that was once normal and cherished will have vanished from view – a victim of changing times, ignorance and apathy.

This blatant deficiency of godly men seems to follow an almost distinct cycle. Starting all the way back in Bible days, progressing through the centuries up to the present, it is clear that there is a noticeable trend. I say noticeable, only because history tends to repeat itself. For the apathetic observer, it may not be so obvious. As generations come and go, there has been a consistent cycle where God-fearing men were prominent and powerful, only to succumb to worldliness, opposition and decay. Any student of history will admit that the rise and fall of nations and empires were directly related to the quality of its men. The ancient empires of Rome and Greece were undermined from within. It was not the swords and spears of outsiders that brought these world conquerors to their knees. It was the corruption, lust, greed and immoral lifestyles of the rulers and male population that ultimately resulted in the ruin of these great civilizations.

America will never be destroyed from the outside.
If we falter and lose our freedoms,
It will be because we destroyed ourselves.
- ***Abraham Lincoln***

England was once a ruler of the sea and land; a nation with world-wide influence. England was the envy of the world, both militarily and economically. It was a place where God worked mightily for many years. Many of its great preachers and evangelists were used of God to spread revival around the world. England sent out many missionaries and was a place where people had an acute awareness of God and the Scriptures. Today, England is a spiritual graveyard. Immorality, liberalism and rampant ungodliness are the norm. The churches are empty, and atheism is growing. Research reveals that only one out of ten greater men of science in the UK even believes there is a God! What are the results of this increasing apostasy? Notice these results from the International Crime Victim Survey. People in England and Wales experienced more crime per head than any other country in the survey, 54.5 crimes per 100 inhabitants compared with an average of 35.2 per 100. People in England and Wales face the second highest risk of being a victim of crime. Australia was the worst with 30% of its people victims of crime in 2000, followed by England and Wales with 26.4%. England and Wales had the worst record for "very serious" offences, scoring 18 for every hundred inhabitants, followed by Australia with 16.

To deny the influence of God-fearing men is to deny reality! The Bible says in Psalms 33:12, "Blessed is the nation whose God is the LORD. . . ." We are seeing this same cause and effect taking place in America. The latest reports indicate that murders and rapes are increasing. The number of abortions, divorces and teen pregnancies are escalating. Mark 3:27 says, "No man can enter into a strong man's house, and spoil his goods, except he will first bind the strong man; and then he will spoil his house." Our strong men have been bound, and our houses are being spoiled. Men have been bound by chains of every description. They have been overpowered and rendered totally useless in the fight against Satanic attacks.

This trend must have existed during the days of King Solomon. He also sensed the increasing carnality of the men around him when he penned these words in Proverbs 20:6, "Most men will proclaim every one his own goodness: but a faithful man who can find?" In the next chapter, we will look at the two kinds of men described in this verse. What I want to draw your attention to in this chapter is the famine of faithful men. You can visualize the urgency and the frustration of Solomon as he asks, "But a faithful man who can find?" I can almost imagine him standing up in his throne room and looking around the palace for someone to fit his description of a faithful man. Maybe he leaned out over the palisade and watched the people of his kingdom walking to and fro. He might have gone and reviewed his troops, searching for that special man. We can only imagine the lengths Solomon went to in his efforts to find a man that he considered to be faithful. Picture his disappointment when he realized that there was a severe shortage of faithful men; men he could depend on. His frustration is evident by his question.

As I endeavor to fulfill my role as a pastor and a preacher of the gospel, I too feel the frustration of looking for faithful men. I realize, of course, that faithful men are developed, not born. However, the soberness of David's assessment is a bit overwhelming at times. In Psalms 12:1, we can hear the Psalmist's cry of anguish as he calls out to God in his desperation. "Help, LORD; for the godly man ceaseth; for the faithful fail from among the children of men." Can you hear his plea? Can you feel his pain? Here is a man that God describes as "a man after mine own heart. . . ." (I Samuel 13:14; Acts 13:22). God was looking for a man that He could go to when He needed a task performed; a man He could approach with anything He needed doing - whether it be a giant that needed defeating or a city that needed destroying. David was that man. He was God's "go-to" man during those days of Israel's existence. David had his faults and he had his character flaws, but he was a man that loved God and wasn't ashamed of it.

Just as David called out to God in his time of frustration, I have also realized that God is the only One that can replenish the earth with godly men. David cried, "Help, Lord…," knowing that God was the only Source of help. What is frightening is this prayer of bewilderment and pain was uttered thousands of years ago! Realize, this was years ago where it was nothing to call for volunteers to go and fight and even die in defense of their God Jehovah and thousands of men would step forward! Can you imagine a leader today asking for volunteers to go and die for the cause of Christ? What a disappointing response he would get! What a small, frail and flimsy army he would find himself with! David's failure to find godly men and his verdict that the 'faithful' had failed from among the children of men would surely be amplified if he were writing Psalms today. Finding a man is difficult enough; not to mention finding a godly man!!

Christian manhood is a complicated topic. It is a subject that covers so much territory that it would take a lifetime to explore it and understand it. It is not so much that the topic of manhood is complicated, but the fact that men are complicated creatures. Women cannot understand us. Our children can't understand us.

What is worse, we sometimes can't understand ourselves! As a man who is a husband, a dad and a God-called preacher, the spiritual condition of men today has become a heavy burden on my heart. Everywhere I go, I encounter men that are hurting. They are suffering from every plague imaginable. Abusive parents, broken homes, unfaithful spouses, rebellious children, sexual lusts, disappointing role models and undefined expectations have left their devastating toll on men everywhere. The inward emotions, the mental warfare, the social pressures and the financial strain have made life unbearable for millions of men. They are reeling from Satanic attacks like never before. Temptations are overwhelming and opportunities to sin are on every hand. Marriages are crumbling; suicides are increasing. The statistics of Christian men that have killed themselves are shocking. What would be even more shocking would be the number of those that have thought about it.

Satan's attack on the home has men completely off balance. Their home is supposed to be their domain, but it feels more like a dungeon. They are locked in a situation they absolutely despise but they cannot find a way out. They cannot control their wife, their children or even themselves. It is like the whole world is in a cyclone with everyone hanging on for dear life while things spin helplessly out of control. They cannot control their destiny, their spending, their debt, their lusts, their mind - nothing!

Everybody is looking at you like you're some kind of superhero. They expect you to just drop what you're doing, put on your cape and fly to the rescue. You would really like to solve all of your problems before tackling everybody else's. You cannot take it anymore, and you are just trying to figure out what went wrong. What did go wrong? Was it meant to be this way? Was this the kind of life God intended for you to live? Does God have an alternative plan that doesn't involve so much confusion and trouble? Is it actually possible to be a man in the 21st century and have it all together? Is Christian manhood a possibility or a paradox?

David: A Man's Man

It has almost gotten to the place where a man with his fair share of testosterone is labeled as aggressive, domineering, chauvinistic, hateful and mean. People are so busy propping up their own agendas and screaming about their rights that they have stripped us men of many of our necessary virtues. I say virtues because a man with guts; with backbone, with a voice, and with the ability to lead is a man of virtue!! I make no apologies for announcing that we are in desperate need of MEN! Manhood is in serious danger of extinction if men do not stand up for what a man is all about. There are some that would redefine manhood, while others just scoff at the concept. In the Christian realm, we need men more than ever. Women's role in the church and in the work of God cannot be minimized, but neither can that of the men.

David was a "man's man". He has always been one of my heroes. He was both a blood-soaked warrior and a passionate lover. He was beheading his enemies one day and writing Psalms the next. He was taking lives with his sword one minute and later encouraging others with his quill. He was a man that was wielding a sling or spear one hour and strumming his harp the next! David was a killer, a fighter and a warrior second to none, yet he was also a husband, father, poet, songwriter, and musician unlike anybody in his time. What a man! No wonder God said he was a man after His own heart. I'm of the persuasion that most people today have no idea what God values in people. They are totally unable to comprehend a God that actually endorsed a man like David. It is becoming easier to understand David's perplexity at his failure to find a faithful and godly man. This is coming from a man that understood both what it meant to be faithful and to be a man!

Try and understand David's upbringing and contrast it with the upbringing of young men today. He was placed in the position of guarding the family flocks at a very early age. The

Bible details his one-on-one confrontations with both a lion and a bear. A modern teenager would have tucked tail and ran, provided he was mature enough to be entrusted with such a responsibility in the first place. David simply took control of the situation and single-handedly conquered both the lion and the bear. In the case of the lion, the Bible says he "went out after him, and smote him, and delivered it out of his mouth: and when he arose against me, I caught him by his beard, and smote him, and slew him" (1 Samuel 17:35).

Can you visualize this scene? David went out after him! He chased down a full grown lion that was hungry enough to attack a flock of sheep with a human being standing nearby. David went after him and smote him, apparently stunning the lion to the extent that David was able to take the poor, no doubt bleeding, lamb out of its mouth. When the lion recovered from David's first assault, he attacked David. David caught him by his beard and smote him again, and then killed him. What a feat! What bravery! What courage!

We can only imagine a scene like this in a movie. For David, this was part of his everyday life. This event, and others similar to it, prepared him for an even more unbelievable feat – that of fighting Goliath of Gath. While all the other men of Israel were trembling in fear, David coolly approached the giant with nothing more than a sling, five smooth stones, and faith in his God. After humiliating and infuriating the renegade giant with threats and taunts, he proceeded to run toward him with his sling swinging furiously overhead. Supernaturally, the stone found its target, and the giant fell face down on the ground. David, having learned his lesson with the lion, didn't walk away and take any chances of this enemy coming back to kill him. He walked over, pulled the giant's huge sword from its sheath, and in front of the eyes of the entire Israeli army and the Philistine army, very efficiently cut off Goliath's head. When the Philistines saw this, they turned in terror and retreated in disarray. As the Israeli soldiers took off in pursuit, David reached down and grabbed Goliath's big bloody head and marched off to claim his reward from Saul.

In today's world, this would be perceived as the gross and perverted display of a psycho. Strangely enough, when David strolled into the city, still carrying this uncircumcised Philistine's head, the people began to sing his praises. David claimed his prize, and events began to unfold that would eventually see him ruling from the throne as the second king of Israel.

Manhood under Attack

Just recently, the latest Superman movie was surrounded by speculation as to Clark Kent's true sexual orientation. FoxNews.com posted an article on June 26, 2006 that began with this statement: "Warner Bros. rolls out a whole new Superman on Wednesday — one who doubts himself, ponders his reason for being, leaves his family and might even be gay, if you believe the Internet buzz." The director, Brian Singer, though a self-professed homosexual himself, vehemently denied Superman's "gayness." He insisted that Clark Kent was a heterosexual, but declared that the "man of steel" was now much more sensitive. Why would a man who is modest enough to conceal his own true identity now be pressured into being even more sensitive? Why must a man that can fly, leap tall buildings and saves thousands of lives be so concerned about his sensitivity? The story line also portrayed Superman as having an identity crisis – not knowing why he is here or who he is. Society's attack on real manhood is blatantly nauseating! Maybe they should have changed his name to Supersissy. You can save the world all you want to, just make sure to be sensitive while you're doing it! Unbelievable!

Another example of society's attack on men is a recent movie starring Meryl Streep, who plays a tyrannical fashion magazine editor in "The Devil Wears Prada." She insists she didn't draw on Vogue editor Anna Wintour for her character -- on the contrary, she based it on men she knows. She went on to say, "Unfortunately you don't have enough women in power, or at least I don't know them, to copy," she said in New York before the film's release. "Most of my models for this character were ... male," she said. We all know that there is not a single woman in the world that is tyrannical, so it makes sense that she had to use men for that role. Streep joked that there was plenty for men to enjoy as well. Asked at a news gathering whether she thought the film's storyline about a tough female boss being successful in the business world made it a feminist movie, she denied it. "There's a way to kill the box office," she said. "No, this is a guy flick, a lot of eye candy, a lot of lingerie shots" *(today.reuters.com/news – June 28, 2006).* Now if a man had made such a remark about a woman, he would be labeled as a sexist in the worst kind of way. Not only are men tyrants, but all they care about is sex! It is so clear to see the message that the world is trying to send – men are not only idiots, they are bossy, unreasonable sex addicts.

When I was doing some research for this book, I ran across a most interesting title for a book. The title was "Take It Like A Man." You can imagine my surprise to discover that the book was the autobiography of Boy George, the homosexual musician from the UK. Suddenly, the title took on an ugly, perverted connotation. Needless to say, I have not read the book and don't plan to. I do not need a make-up wearing sodomite telling me anything about being a man!

The Death of Manliness

Our society has eroded to where weak, effeminate men are looked upon with respect and admiration. We are constantly being told that instead of focusing on who we are and our mission in life, we need to be focusing on people's perception of us and making those around us feel loved, accepted and equal. On the other hand, a man that has a strong constitution, leadership qualities and the courage to go with it is regarded with disdain and disgust and perceived to be a threat to the well being of others. A man is more apt to be rebuked for carrying a gun than a purse. We are living in the days when a man that shoots a deer is abused while a man that kills his neighbor is acquitted. It is acceptable for a boy to wear earrings and necklaces, [but God forbid he carry a pocket knife!] Men have been carrying, using, and collecting weapons of every description since the beginning of time. Today, a man that has a gun or any other weapon is ridiculed for his "lack of faith" or is berated by the world as a danger to society. It seems that they failed to read the words of the Lord Jesus Christ in Luke 22:36 when He said, "… he that hath no sword, let him sell his garment, and buy one." How can it be immoral to carry a weapon if Christ commanded His disciples to carry one, even if they had to sell their clothes to buy it? Again, the world is scared to death of a man with a gun. Cain didn't have a gun, but that didn't stop him from killing his brother. Mind you, Cain had never even heard of murder. He had never seen a violent movie or played a violent video game. Guns do not kill people; people kill people. Murder is a heart problem, not a weapon problem.

    The unbelieving world has many misconceptions of Christ. They see the paintings of Him with pale, smooth skin; long hair; and long eyelashes. They see a weak, impotent sissy. Their perception of Christ is so unrealistic. He was not a sissy. He was not pale. He didn't have long hair. He was a MAN! He lived outdoors most of the time, so He couldn't have been pale. He overthrew the moneychangers in the temple, armed only with a homemade whip, so He couldn't have been a sissy. He outright condemned long hair on a man in I Corinthians 11, so He couldn't have worn His hair long. Furthermore, to endure the scourging and the beatings, to carry the cross out of the city of Jerusalem and up the mountain, and still live several more hours on that cross were not the deeds of a wimp or a sissy. Jesus Christ was a man of unbelievable courage, strength and stamina. Make no mistake about it! No doubt, the 30 years he had worked in and around a carpenter's shop had made Him physically fit. He was definitely not a weak, sickly man.

The world system has for the past five decades slowly strangled what little bit of manhood was still alive almost completely out of our male population. Teenagers today can plug in and operate an X-Box, but they can't clean a fish. They can figure out Nintendo, but they can't figure out how to start a lawn mower. They can change hair styles every two weeks, but they couldn't change the oil in the car if their life depended on it! They faint at the sight of blood. They cry at the first sign of a blister. They can't work for longer than 20 minutes without a break. They are pampered and babied long after adolescence. They are spoiled, weak and timid. They can't resist temptations; they can't defend themselves or their belongings.

They are plagued with a victim mentality and are easily intimidated. They shy away from strong male influences and cling to the women and younger siblings in their life. They have to go places in groups because they can't face the world alone. They can't get a job; and if they do, they can't keep it. They have no respect for authority, and have no idea how to exert it. The world owes them everything, and they are not responsible for anything they have or anything they do. If they own anything, it was given to them or it was begged, borrowed or stolen. They have no concept of work, earning wages, spending those wages on necessities, or paying their own way. The teens of today are more experienced in making babies than they are in making a budget. They can find time to pamper themselves, shop, buy music and party, but they can't find the time to pay for their own room and board.

The list goes on, but who is at fault in this fiasco? Who is to blame for this gross distortion of life? We can blame the young men, but they are a product of their environment and their upbringing. They are exactly what they were trained to be

– parasites. Society, entertainment, Hollywood and the parents have taught them that God's roles for men and women are outdated. The world has determined that the lines of demarcation between a real woman and a real man should be obliterated. They have blurred the distinction so effectively that our children are growing up with a perverted sense of reality and identity. This is evident by the growing number of self-professed lesbians and homosexuals. What God calls an abomination has been crammed down the throats of society, making anyone that protests appear to be from another planet. Being politically correct has taken preeminence over being Biblically correct.

What happened to the days when the men were admired for their strength and women for her virtues? What happened to the days where the husband was the one that brought home the bacon and the wife was glad to cook it and serve it? What happened to God's ordained plan of the woman to bear children and the man to sweat and labor for their food? Nowadays, women want to bear the kids and support them. Many men are content to sit at home and let them.

Damsels in Distress

We could all no doubt provide a long list of young Christian women that are searching for a husband. As they exit their twenty's and enter into their thirty's, they began to panic. They have patiently waited for God to send them a man, but there just are not any out there. They've prayed and asked God to fulfil their innate desire to share their life and their love with someone who will assume the proper role of spiritual leader in the home and be a shoulder they can lean on. However, as the years pass, hope and anticipation slowly turn into fear, anxiety and hopelessness. The shortage of faithful men is setting the stage for a major crisis in the upcoming generation. The noticeable absence of exceptional men has resulted in women settling for just any man. What began as an ambitious search for "Mr. Right" has deteriorated into a half-hearted satisfaction at finding "Mr. OK." Why? Because knights in shining armor are as extinct as the fire breathing dragons they hunt. There are plenty of damsels in distress, but no real men to come to their rescue. Christian women today have such high hopes in finding a godly husband. They desire a man that is saved, serves God, has a decent job, and will treat them like a lady. Exceptional? You better believe it!

When godly women cannot find godly men to marry, they are faced with two choices. They can either remain unmarried and die alone and childless, or they can compromise their convictions and marry an ungodly man to meet that physical desire for companionship. Either choice is a less-than-attractive one. Either option is bound to have a negative effect on Christianity in the years to come. The woman that chooses to remain unmarried will unfortunately forfeit the hope of ever raising God-fearing children and making some long lasting contribution to the work of God.

The woman that chooses to marry out of the will of God will at best be entering into a life of turmoil and disagreement as to the proper training of her children. Children coming from broken homes or homes with unsaved fathers have little or no chance to ever establish a godly home of their own. The shortage of faithful men in the home is enough in itself to provoke Christians everywhere to action. As goes the home, so goes the church; and as goes the church, so goes the nation. The fact that common men grossly outnumber exceptional men is setting the stage for major problems in our country.

God is Looking for a Man

One of the saddest verses in the Bible is found in Ezekiel 22:30. "<u>And I sought for a man among them</u>, that should make up the hedge, and stand in the gap before me for the land, that I should not destroy it: <u>but I found none</u>." We have already discussed David's frustration at not being able to find a faithful man, but here we see God couldn't find one either! In the whole nation of Israel, there was not a man that God could entrust with the responsibility of filling the gap in the wall. How sad! For some reason, the wall of protection has been damaged. It was either a result of neglect, attack or poor construction. Whatever the case, the purpose of the wall was being compromised. The primary purpose of a wall is for separation and protection. It keeps out what is supposed to stay out, and it keeps in what is supposed to stay in. Now get the picture. Here is a wall, with a gap in it. God has searched for a man to stand in that gap and fulfil the purpose of the wall. He wants a man that will enforce separation and provide protection. The sad part is He couldn't find A SINGLE MAN to do it!

In the following chapters, we will examine the Biblical expectations of a man and his role in the work of God. I might add that God is STILL looking for a man! God is looking for a man of character and integrity that He can appoint to perform a specific task. He is searching for men that can accomplish His plan and His purpose in this world.

God is Looking For A Man

When God endeavors to find a man,
    He has a certain Sovereign plan.
He does not call just anyone,
    but one who will get His perfect will done.

First He looks for one who is clean and pure,
    and lives a life that is right and sure.
Who knows the meaning of holiness
    and walks each day in His perfect rest.

For God cannot use a dirty, unclean vessel;
    one who views a holy life as a chore and a hassle.
But rather He chooses those in love with Him;
    who attempts to stay clean and close to Him.

God also looks for men filled with boldness and courage;
    who do not withdraw in the face of Satan's fury.
For a God-called man will ruffle some feathers,
    and he must endure through all kinds of weather.

There's plenty who'll love him when his preaching is positive,
    but that crowd disappears when he tells them how to live.
His members will accuse him of being too bold,
    yet they wonder why their hearts are so dead and cold.

They accuse him of running prospective members away
    by not closing his eyes to their worldly play.
A man who desires to be used of the Lord
    must also be confident and sure in his words.

For God cannot use a man who is in doubt;
    who talks of a God he knows nothing about!
A servant of God must be sure in his belief
    and have enough power to bring sinners to their knees.

We're to study to show ourselves approved unto Him
    and not spend all our time playing ball in the gym!
And the final requirement that God's looking for
    is a man who is committed in his walk with the Lord.

He's aware the world's watching his every move
    and has a desire for God's will to prove.
He watches his language, his actions, his life
    and sets the example before his kids and his wife.

*Some will say he's too hard and has no compassion,
    because he is selective in choosing companions.
But the life of the godly is one that is serious
    and the world may say that you're strange and your curious.*

*But just remember the rewards of living for Him,
    and the terrible fate that's waiting for them.
So why don't you live like you know you ought to;
    who knows but someday, maybe God will use you?*

By M. S. Shiflett

Chapter Three

The Exceptional Man versus the Common Man

"Most men will proclaim every one his own goodness: but a faithful man who can find?" (Proverbs 20:6)

Ex·cep·tion·al - *adj. 1. Being an exception; uncommon. 2. Well above average; extraordinary 3. Deviating widely from a norm, as of physical or mental ability.*

What constitutes an exceptional man? When I look around, I realize that most men are unexceptional. They may be cordial, hard working and even clever at times. Nevertheless, they are quite ordinary. They all have so many things in common that it is impossible to not perceive them as common. What qualities in a man would place him in a higher percentile? What traits would render him above average? What exactly should a man strive for in order to rise above the multitudes around him? As a young boy, there were men in my life that stood head and shoulders above the rest. From an early age I wanted to be like them. I wanted my life to be more than just the norm. I wanted to experience a closer walk with God and to impact lives on a daily basis. I did not want to just fit in with the crowd and go through life being normal. I wanted more.

Many men have strange ideas about what makes a man superior. Some think it is size. Some of the greatest men in history were not men of great stature. Some might feel that it is physical strength and fitness. That is also a myth. Many great men were physically disadvantaged and even sickly. Money sure isn't the solution. In fact, there's nothing that can spoil a man faster than wealth. The Bible declares that the love of money is the root of all evil. An exceptional lust for material riches is certainly not the trademarks of an exceptional man. So what makes a man exceptional?

As I look around, I have discovered at least three major ingredients that are missing in the lives of most men. The three adjectives that describe a man that is exceptional are bold, balanced and Biblical. To find a man with one of these traits may not be that difficult. To find a man with two of these characteristics would be even harder. To find a man with all three of these attributes is without a doubt exceptional.

The Bold Man

"The wicked flee when no man pursueth: but the righteous are bold as a lion."
(Proverbs 28:1)

If there is any character flaw that is more disgusting than cowardice, I do not know what it is. I am amazed on a daily basis at men that simply lock up in the face of conflict or adversity. They sweat. They squirm. They tug at their collar. They blush. They fall apart. The slightest confrontation has them so unnerved that they can hardly function. They blame their lack of courage on everything under the sun, but they can't seem to get a grip on it. I've seen big, strong men nearly wet themselves over the slightest provocation. I have watched men reduced to mush under the tirades of an angry woman.

In their effort not to be labeled a bully, many men have surrendered every ounce of backbone that God gave them. I have no problem acknowledging that if there is no middle ground between a bully and a coward, I'll choose being a bully any day of the week. Fortunately there is a middle ground. What we need today is more men that will put on their britches and stand up for what is right without worrying what everybody will think of them. If you need to sprinkle some gunpowder in your cereal to get you going, then do it. It is time for men to become men again. It is time for men to raise their boys to be men. We are raising a generation of soft, wimpy, delicate, fragile boys. Our boys are subjected to the influence of a dominating mother and a spineless father, and the end result is the politically correct, tree hugging, liberal, peace-loving wackos we have running around today.

I will go a step further. As the boldness of men has deteriorated, the homosexual statistics have risen. I am thoroughly convinced that the lack of bold, balanced and Biblical men has contributed to the rise in perversion. Weak men produce weaker men. Men have allowed both women and children to rob them of their God-given role as a man. They are easily intimidated. They wilt under threats. They have no idea what it means to put their foot down. I have even heard of men that woke up in the night hearing sounds in the house, and sent their wife to investigate! They are scared of guns. They're scared of the dark. They're scared of everything. They can't stand up to their family when it comes to raising the children for God. They can't stand up to their wife. I have even seen women tell their husbands to shut up and sit down, and he does it!

When the world mocks them, they shrivel up and faint. They can't live a public testimony for fear someone will laugh at them. They won't pray over their food in public for worrying about what somebody might say. They lie and retreat when they are confronted about their beliefs. They cannot stand alone

because they feel too vulnerable. Our society is plagued with men who have no idea what being bold is all about.
If their boss asks them to work on Sunday, they will. They are more afraid of losing their job or making the boss mad than they are standing up for what is right. If their daughter wants to date an earring-wearing slob, they let her. If the son comes in late with the family car, Dad will say nothing. He hasn't got the guts. He can't handle the pressure. He's a coward.

We could go on for ever about this matter of boldness if we only used Bible characters for examples. How much boldness do you think it took Noah to preach to that wicked crowd in his day? What about Moses before Pharaoh? What about Daniel before his king when he was discovered praying? The men in the Bible that come to mind that exemplified boldness and courage are too many to enumerate. Paul encouraged the men in the church at Corinth to buckle up and get some boldness. "Watch ye, stand fast in the faith, quit you like men, be strong" (1 Corinthians 16:13).

When David approached the battle scene and saw his brethren and the Israelite army trembling in fear at Goliath's threats, he asked a simple question. He asked them what would be done to the man that defeated the giant. David's own brethren turned on him with these railing accusations. "Why camest thou down hither? and with whom hast thou left those few sheep in the wilderness? I know thy pride, and the naughtiness of thine heart; for thou art come down that thou mightest see the battle" (II Samuel 17:28). No doubt, David expected that. He was ready with his answer. "And David said, What have I now done? Is there not a cause?" (vs. 29) He didn't let their false perception of his courage intimidate him or restrain him from doing what needed to be done. People may criticize you for your boldness. That's fine. Let them. They may call you an arrogant, cocky bully. That's OK too. If you are, get right with God. If you're not, let it go in one ear and out the other.

Boldness and courage is an extremely vital character trait. God says the righteous will be bold as a lion. When you read your Bible, one common denominator of all the great men listed was that they were men of courage. Courage is not the absence of fear; courage is doing what needs to be done in spite of it. To fear is human; to run is cowardice.

The Balanced Man

"Let me be weighed in an even balance, that God may know mine integrity." (Job 31:6)

The most difficult thing to find in people today is balance. You do not hear much about it, but balance is such a missing element in society. It seems that everybody is going to extremes. Finding a balanced man is definitely out of the ordinary. God's word has a lot to say about being balanced. A balanced man is a well-rounded man. It is easy to find men that are involved in some kind of hobby or sport or job that dominates their life. They neglect their family. They neglect the Lord. They neglect their church. They neglect their responsibilities. All they can think about is their favorite pastime or their work.

An example of this is the story of the two men that were golfing one Saturday. As they were about to tee off, a funeral procession drove by. The older man stopped and took his hat off and placed it over his heart until the last car had driven by. Then he put his hat back on and commenced to tee off. The younger man looked at him with awe and said, "Sir, that was about the most decent thing I've seen anybody do in a long time." The old man shrugged and said, "Well, it was the least I could do. I was married to her for forty years!"

It is a shame that so many men are known for their vices or their hobbies or their jobs. They get all wrapped up in their own little world and they forget everything else. There is no balance in their life. There is a place for hobbies and enjoyment, but there is also a place for God. There is a place for work and careers, but what about your family? So many men are completely one-dimensional. They can only focus on one thing at the time. It is either their job or nothing. It is either sports or nothing. Their world is so small that there is not enough room for others and their needs. Juggling the many tasks of a career, a husband, a father, a friend, a mentor, a neighbor and a Christian takes some thought and planning. Having discipline and order in a chaotic world is vitally important to your influence as a man. Learning how to multi-task without leaving things undone is quite a chore.

What it all boils down to basically is that an unbalanced man is a selfish man. He is a simple man. He is immature and uncaring. To leave important areas of your life unattended because you have "something else to do" is harmful. It hurts relationships. It will hurt everyone around you if you are not careful to properly disperse your attention. Unfortunately, if any area gets neglected, it is usually the most important areas such as Bible reading, prayer, church attendance, quality time with the kids, or a quiet date with the wife. Why is it that the sports, the TV watching, the goofing off with the guys and carnal things never seem to get neglected? Why is it you always have time for those things, and not the important things? Why does God or family have to always be the first ones to take a back seat when things start to get hectic?

Being balanced is something that requires effort and planning. It will not just happen by accident. As a pastor, I have more work to do than I can ever accomplish. My days are full of ministry work that includes, but is not limited to, visiting church members, preparing messages, writing, praying, planning outreaches and overseeing a church with a Christian Academy, a Boy's Home, and hosting a Camp Meeting twice a year. Most days I run non-stop from early morning until late at night. The work of a pastor is never done. Somewhere in the middle of all that, I have a wife that needs a husband. I have four little children that need a daddy. I have people from the community or from the church dropping by unannounced all throughout the day. People call and want help and need counseling. It can become very overwhelming at times. Finding time to go for a jog or shoot some basketball just to get the "ole" heart pumping is rare. I own a nice set of golf clubs and I love to play, but it has been two years since I had the opportunity. The grass keeps growing and needs cutting. The leaves keep falling and need raking. The car needs washing and the truck needs an oil change. The dog needs to go to the vet for something and the list just goes on. If you are not careful, you will find yourself in a selfish slump; only doing what you want to do and letting everything else just go to pot. A balanced man is indeed an exceptional man.

The Biblical Man

"All scripture is given by inspiration of God, and is profitable for doctrine, for reproof, for correction, for instruction in righteousness:
That the man of God may be perfect, throughly furnished unto all good works."
(II Timothy 3:16, 17)

The Bible is an amazing book. It is without a doubt the most loved, the most hated, the most cherished, the most neglected, the most quoted and misquoted book of all time. It is the foundation for every truth, and also used as the basis for every cult, false religion and heresy imaginable. It is the object of unity and fellowship as well as division and debate. It has been said that the two topics one should never discuss are religion and politics. The Bible is the most misunderstood book of its main proponents of any textbook known to man. An English professor will memorize his textbooks. I had a history professor in college that could literally quote the entire history book: dates, names and details. Why is it that professing Bible-believers do not know their Bible?

Biblical ignorance is not just a problem; it is a plague. Christians do not know their Bible. Men that profess to know God and to believe His word know very little about it. They know just enough about it to make themselves look stupid if a discussion comes up. Finding a man that knows his Bible is extremely rare. I will go a step further. There are not too many men that are in the ministry that know their Bible. They spent all their time in seminary studying everything under the sun except their Bible.

Near our home while we were in South Africa was a University where I had the opportunity to address the students on several occasions. The Theological Department of that school has just announced that they will be offering a full term of classes on John Calvin. I was completely bewildered. Why in heaven's name would a Theological Department offer classes on a human being that was born sixteen hundred years after the Bible was completed? Why would they not study the life of Christ, Paul, the disciples or someone found in the Bible? This is no doubt the very crowd that God was referring to when He declared that there would be those that are "Ever learning, and never able to come to the knowledge of the truth" (II Timothy 3:7). You can know everything there is to know about John Calvin, but that will not further your understanding of Scripture one iota!

Just recently, Leon, one of the young men in South Africa that attends the church I founded got into a discussion about pedo-baptism with a retired Dutch Reformed minister. During the discussion, Leon asked the pastor for Biblical evidence for the teaching that babies should be sprinkled. The minister admitted that there was no record of such a practice in the Scriptures. Leon began to talk to him about the errors of infant baptism and showed him from the Bible what God's word says about baptism. He carefully detailed from Scripture that baptism must be performed only on those that have a clear testimony of salvation and it must be done in deep water by immersion. The retired minister eventually remarked to Leon, "I'll have to admit, you know your Bible better than I do." The sad thing is that Leon had only been saved for a few months. Here he was walking circles around a man that had stood behind the pulpit for nearly fifty years but did not know his Bible! This is exactly what Jesus was talking about when He asked the question, "Can the blind lead the blind? shall they not both fall into the ditch?" (Luke 6:39)

As a pastor, there is not a week that goes by that I do not challenge my people to "search the scriptures." I realize that I am human, and to be a human is to make mistakes. I am not perfect and don't profess to be. However, there is one thing that is perfect. That is the word of God. It is the Final Authority for all matters of faith and practice. If as a man I am going to please God, I must know His word! I must live by the principles and precepts laid out in the Scriptures. To fail to know God's word and to live by it is to fail as a man and as a Christian. "Thy word is a lamp unto my feet, and a light unto my path" (Psalms 119:105). To live your life without first consulting God's word is like going hiking through a dark forest at night without a lantern. "The way of the wicked is as darkness: they know not at what they stumble" (Proverbs 4:19).

I determined many years ago that I would try my best to be as Biblical as I possibly could. My wife and my children must understand that to obey God is our first and foremost responsibility. If God's word teaches it, we must do it. If God's word forbids it, we must not do it. Following God and His plan for our lives is the only way we can be assured of a happy, blessed and fruitful existence. Too many people are making reckless choices. They make up their mind according to their desires or personal tastes. That is a huge mistake. "There is a way that seemeth right unto a man, but the end thereof are the ways of death" (Proverbs 16:25). Learn your Bible and live by your Bible. That would definitely qualify you as an exceptional man.

The Foolish Man

"... lovers of pleasures more than lovers of God;"
(II Timothy 3:4)

In a society that makes gods of men with superior athletic ability, the fact that there is a shortage of godly men seems to escape us. We can name long lists of superstars that excel in the various fields of sports. We keep up with the scores and the statistics and can even give a running record of their past achievements and career highlights. In a world where a man's ability to throw or hit or catch a ball is elevated to abnormal, unrealistic heights, who has time to be godly? Who has time to be faithful? Who cares about doing anything of eternal value?

The major league sports world pays millions of dollars per year to entice men to be all they can be in their particular field of expertise. They promote them, push them on the public and esteem them as some sort of true hero. Many of them are illiterate. They have never worked a full day on a real job of any description. They are a bunch of spoiled, immoral braggarts, yet they receive adoration and accolades from everybody. They are worshipped in the cathedrals and temples of their stadiums and ballparks. Their wicked lifestyles are excused and ignored. Several of them in recent years have been acquitted of unbelievable crimes and accusations. Even with overwhelming evidence, the public judges and juries proclaim these sports gods completely innocent. Their checkered past only serves to increase their popularity and ego.

These men seem to be invincible and unstoppable. Breaking records and outdoing someone else becomes their driving ambition, and while they are attempting this, they are being cheered on by their blind, biased worshippers. The use of steroids, though illegal according to the rules of the game, is flagrantly flaunted and excused by the fans. While the old timers are worried about the integrity of the game being compromised, where is the concern about the more important issues? Who is heralding the need for men with character, morals and a significant contribution to society?

Many people to some extent enjoy sports and keep up with what is going on, but let's be honest: it is all vanity. The time, the money and the energy spent on sports is such a waste! None of it holds any eternal value. The awards, the trophies, the headlines and the attention do nothing to better anyone's life - in either this life or the life to come. The Bible clearly commands us in Ephesians 5:16 to be busy "redeeming the time, because the days are evil." How can we justify the time and money we spend on this nonsense?

The headlines are filled with news pertaining to celebrities on a daily basis. We are bombarded with insignificant, useless information about movie stars, actors, singers, and a host of other people that have managed someway to finagle their way into the public eye. Their vices are glorified; their quirks are imitated. Their idiosyncrasies are viewed as normal behavior. Their respective field or career is many times used as an opportunity to promote their own ideas, religion, values (or lack of them) and agendas. (Since when does the fact that a man is a good actor qualify him to publicly analyze foreign policy?)

One recent news item was the absurd piece about Brad Pitt being named by Newsweek magazine as "one of the 15 people that makes America great." Great? In what way? He left his first wife for another woman. They had an illegitimate child together in an expensive, elite resort in Namibia, Africa. He has made millions of dollars acting in R-rated movies filled with profanity, nudity, killing, violence and every kind of ungodliness. How has he made America great? How has a man that has glamorized adultery, divorce, illegitimate childbirth and fornication made America great? He hasn't. The problem is we are seeing the prophecy in Isaiah 5:20 fulfilled right before our eyes. "Woe unto them that call evil good, and good evil; that put darkness for light, and light for darkness; that put bitter for sweet, and sweet for bitter!"

These celebrities and sports heroes are exalted and placed on the highest of pedestals, but what recognition does the godly man receive? When was the last time you were inspired by a public figure to be more like Christ? How would a list of sports heroes and newsmakers compare to a list of faithful men? When it comes to role models in the area of true Christianity, how many men would fit the bill?

Chapter Four

The Exceptional Man's Godliness

"But thou, O man of God, flee these things; and follow after righteousness, godliness, faith, love, patience, meekness." (I Timothy 6:11)

God's definition of godliness is quite clear in the Scriptures. David lamented the fact that "…the godly man ceaseth." In an age when God spoke audibly, and His will could not be mistaken, men were still slow to conform to God's expectations. It is even more rare today to find a man that can be honestly referred to as "godly". We often hear men described as honest, hard-working, kind, athletic, strong or even referred to as a "good father" or a "good husband," but when was the last time you referred to a man as "godly"? If the truth were known, a lot of men wouldn't even desire to be described in that manner. Maybe they have this perception of a "godly man" being an old, white-haired, retired pastor that gets up every morning at four o'clock and prays for an hour. Children can be godly. Teenagers can be godly. Young dads and newlyweds can be godly! It is not a shameful thing to be godly!

Godly Actions

When God gave the command to be godly, He was talking to everybody – men included! Paul told Timothy in 1 Timothy 6:11, "But thou, O man of God, flee these things; and follow after righteousness, godliness, faith, love, patience, meekness." It should be our earnest desire to follow after God's standard of godliness. Becoming godly will be a process that will only take place if undertaken on purpose. You will never be defined by others as a "godly" man unless you make a deliberate attempt to be one. Paul's advice involved two basic rules: flee and follow. In order to follow after godliness, there are some things you will have to flee! Just as Joseph fled from the seductive enticements of Potiphar's wife, you too will find yourself having to flee certain things and situations.

The godly man will be godly in his actions. His life will demonstrate character and integrity. The Apostle Peter encouraged men to be godly with his exhortation in II Peter 3:11, "Seeing then that all these things shall be dissolved, what manner of persons ought ye to be in all holy conversation and godliness." The word "conversation" in that verse means lifestyle, conduct or behavior. A man's behavior is a direct reflection of his heart and soul. What is on the inside will be manifested by your actions. Proper actions may not always mean a godly heart, but a godly heart will always result in godly actions.

As men, we have been encouraged to be godly. We've also been empowered to be godly. "According as his divine power hath given unto us all things that pertain unto life and godliness. . . " (II Peter 1:3). With the completion of the Scriptures, and the sending of the Comforter, we are completely equipped to live a godly life. There is no reason why a man that has access to the word of God has to live in confusion to God's expectations concerning holiness and godliness. God has clearly defined what is right and wrong in His word. The problem with men today is not the fact that they don't know God's will; the problem is they don't accept God's will! If a man has been born again, he has dwelling within him the Holy Spirit. Jesus explained that one of the ministries of the Holy Spirit is to guide us on our way. "Howbeit when he, the Spirit of truth, is come, he will guide you into all truth. . . " (John 16:13). A man that has the Holy Spirit and the word of God should not be in doubt concerning God's will for his life. God's standards and His expectations are both simple and numerous.

More Like Him

The mercy of Jesus Christ my Lord is something to be considered,
    For when we disobey His Word, rarely is harsh punishment rendered.
My prayer from day to day is this: That I should love Him more,
    And not take for granted His mercy and grace like I once did before.

I also refuse to neglect His Word which melted my heart of stone,
    And too His precious blood was shed for the sins of man to atone.
Longsuffering is another of God's traits to which I oft compare,
    And find that many a problem would disappear if bathed in prayer.

His gentleness, His forbearance, His willingness to forgive,
    Shames me when I recall how worldly I sometimes live.
Oh to be more like my Savior, with His great love for the world,
    And to have His richest blessings from His storehouse above unfurled.
Oh to be more like my Savior, whose example doth truly suffice,
    For not only do I love Him, but I've been bought with the price!

By M. S. Shiflett

Sexual Purity

Godly actions include sexual purity. One of Satan's most effective weapons against men today is in the area of sexual lusts. For the teenager, his daily battle involves immoral girls that are constantly tempting him to sin. Peer pressure and the feats of his friends are daily intimidations that he must learn to overcome. For the single man, moral purity is an even more challenging battle. With freedom and financial growth come stronger temptations. Unlike the days when he was a teenager living at home, he now has a job and many times his own place. That privacy and that freedom offer many new opportunities to gratify one's urges and desires. There is a lack of accountability that makes giving in to temptation so much easier.

The married man also finds himself a target. It is a common misconception among young single men that marriage alleviates immoral temptations. The truth is, once a man is married, and that flame of sexual activity has been ignited, the temptations and satanic devices abound! Just because someone is married does not mean that they are immune to the wiles of the devil. The Scriptures are filled with many examples of great men that were victims of their lusts. Pornography is everywhere. The internet is a source of indescribable filth. Women's morals are more loose than ever before. Sexuality is shoved in our faces on a daily basis. Magazines at the checkout counter feature unbelievable covers. Radio commercials, television shows and even billboards on the side of the road are filled with promiscuity and nudity and sexual innuendos.

A man that is godly in his actions must be determined to remain sexually pure in spite of Satan's onslaught. Job said in Job 31:1, "I made a covenant with mine eyes; why then should I think upon a maid?" In order to remain godly, a man must learn to control his eyes and his mind. When a lustful thought enters your mind, you must learn to cast it down. "Casting down imaginations, and every high thing that exalteth itself against the knowledge of God, and bringing into captivity every thought to the obedience of Christ;" (II Corinthians 10:5). Learning to control your eyes and your mind will be a tremendous step toward maintaining a godly life.

Godly Attitude

Much could be said about a godly man's attitude. Finding the balance between a godly attitude and a necessary attitude is sometimes difficult. When I speak of a necessary attitude, I'm referring to the need to sometimes enforce a decision that may be unpopular. Many times people will accuse you of having an ungodly attitude when in actuality you are doing what you have to do. For example, when Jesus overturned the tables of the moneychangers and ran them out of the Temple, His attitude was not His main concern! His zeal for the house of God overruled His zeal to give a good impression. Sometimes a man is faced with a choice; make a right decision or make a good impression. Many times people will disagree with your decision and will protest its validity by attacking your attitude. Don't get me wrong. A good attitude should be a priority. Portraying the right spirit and possessing a good demeanor is a worthy goal of every man. David prayed in Psalms 51:10, "Create in me a clean heart, O God; and renew a right spirit within me." This is without a doubt a valid prayer and one we should pray daily. However, many men's decisions are based on people's perception of them, rather than on principle.

A godly attitude is not one of weakness. Many times meekness is viewed by the world as weakness. It is possible to make difficult decisions without being difficult. It is possible to make tough choices without acting tough. It is possible to make a true statement without biting a person's head off. Jesus preached truth, but He did it in love. Preaching and teaching and witnessing can be very effective if it is done in the right spirit. There are few things more repulsive than a man that tells somebody that they are lost and going to hell, and he says it as if he wants them to! People do not respond favorably to that kind of approach. They are more readily acceptable of your message if your attitude is one that radiates God's love.

Many times you can be completely Spirit-filled and still make people angry. This fact is illustrated by the life of Stephen. In the book of Acts chapter seven, we are told at least four times that Stephen was filled with the Holy Ghost. This means he was absolutely controlled by the Holy Spirit. He preached a much needed message that was 100% truth. What was the result of his preaching? The Bible says that "when they heard these things, they were cut to the heart, and they gnashed on him with their teeth" (Acts 7:54). Was his attitude wrong? Impossible!! He was filled with the Holy Ghost. Was his message received? No! The moral of this story is very simply this: a true test of your attitude is not the response of the people, but rather the witness of the Spirit within you.

If you have done your best to exemplify a godly attitude and people still do not listen to you or receive your message, then so be it. Just remember these encouraging words of advice from I Peter 3:16: "Having a good conscience; that, whereas they speak evil of you, as of evildoers, they may be ashamed that falsely accuse your good conversation in Christ. For it is better, if the will of God be so, that ye suffer for well doing, than for evil doing."

A Godly Attitude on the Job

Other examples of a godly attitude are found in the employee/employer relationships. Whether you are the boss or you sweep the floor, a godly attitude is commanded by God. No matter who you are or what you do, we are given clear instruction in the Bible about how to act. "Servants, be obedient to them that are your masters according to the flesh, with fear and trembling, in singleness of your heart, as unto Christ; Not with eyeservice, as menpleasers; but as the servants of Christ, doing the will of God from the heart; With good will doing service, as to the Lord, and not to men: Knowing that whatsoever good thing any man doeth, the same shall he receive of the Lord, whether he be bond or free. And, ye masters, do the same things unto them, forbearing threatening: knowing that your Master also is in heaven; neither is there respect of persons with him" (Ephesians 6:5-9).

God's word clearly shows that your attitude toward your boss or your employees is a direct reflection of your attitude toward God. Everything we do is to be motivated by our love for Christ. If you have an unreasonable and unfair boss, keep it to yourself. Your attitude should be one of respect and loyalty as long as you work for him. If the situation is too difficult to bear, then find another job. But to continue to work for a man and dishonor him and disrespect him is an attitude that contradicts God's word. I have had the misfortune of working for men that were complete heathens. Their personality or their mistreatment of their employees was absolutely intolerable. If I couldn't reason with them, I simply walked away. It would be wrong to sow discord behind their back. It would not be right to try and get the others to choose sides or see it your way. It was always helpful to me to remember that when I labor, I am laboring for God. He sees my hard work, and He knows my heart. Even if man doesn't appreciate it, God does! Keep the right attitude on the job in spite of the attitudes of others. That's being godly!

God's instruction to the employer is also quite plain. The Bible says to "forbear threatening." This is a favorite pastime of many bosses. They enjoy making men tremble in fear. They enjoy pulling rank on them and threatening them with the possibility of getting fired. God forbids that kind of attitude. As a Christian employer, you should lead by example – not by threats. Men that run a business or a company with that kind of attitude will not have a loyal following. Those that work for them will simply tolerate them or be constantly looking for another job. Interestingly, God's instruction to the masters reminds them that they also have a Master in heaven! In other words, what goes around comes around! God also makes mention of the fact that with God there is no respect of persons. What He is saying has a double meaning. First of all, just because you're <u>a</u> boss doesn't mean you're <u>the</u> boss! Secondly, just because you are the boss doesn't give you the right to treat people like second class citizens. The people under you have feelings. Treat them with respect, and God will honor your godly attitude.

Before going full-time in the ministry, I was in the construction industry. I operated my own company for about four years. I started working in construction when I was sixteen years old. I started working for a man in my church that owned a drywall business. I worked every day after school helping him hang sheetrock. I enjoyed it, but that man had the meanest attitude! He was fun to be around when we weren't working, but as soon as it was time to make money, he morphed into a tyrant! He was a huge man, with tattoos on his arms. He professed to be saved, but his former life as a drug dealer and cocaine addict had marred his life in many ways. It was like working for Dr. Jekyll and Mr. Hyde! I learned early on to keep my mouth shut and to do what I was told! I distinctly remember one of the worst parts of working for him. He always set the scaffolds up to fit him. He was at least eighteen inches taller than me. When we were nailing the sheetrock to the ceiling, he could hold his end of the board up with his head and use both hands to nail with. Me, I had to hold up the board with one arm and try and start a nail and hammer it with the other hand! How frustrating! About the time I would get my nail started, he would bang on his end of the board and make my nail fall out! Working for him built a lot of character in my life, but he liked to have killed me! After a few months of working for him, I began scouting around for another job. Needless to say, as soon as I found one, I took it. I vowed to always respect the "little people" in my life after that. It is not always about you – it is also about others.

Chapter Five

The Exceptional Man's Gumption

"Whatsoever thy hand findeth to do, do it with thy might;"
(Ecclesiastes 9:10)

Gump·tion - noun - 1. *"boldness of enterprise; initiative or aggressiveness; guts; spunk, common sense."*

    One of the most frustrating elements of manhood is not being able to do something that you need to do. No matter how big or small the crisis, as a man, we are supposed to be able to fix it. We are expected by the women and the children around us to solve the problem quickly and efficiently. Even if it is something we have no experience at, ignorance is not an excuse. We must do something. Anything! We must make a plan and fix whatever needs fixing. It is a direct reflection on our manhood, our intelligence, our role as leaders and heroes. Right? I'm often reminded of the cartoon of a man and a woman driving down the road in their car. Fire is pouring out from under the hood, and car parts are flying everywhere. The woman is looking with great apprehension at her husband, who continues to drive nonchalantly while saying, "It's supposed to do that!" Men don't have the luxury of panic or confusion.

We're always supposed to have the answer to everything! If a crisis arises, it is just understood that we can solve it. No matter what. And usually within five minutes.

How many times have we seen a woman broke down on the side of road with her car parked on the shoulder? Whether it is a flat tire or it is overheated, she needs help. As she walks back and forth, wringing her hands, she's in desperate need of someone to help her. Preferably a man. More particularly, a man that can fix her problem. I've stopped to help them several times and not once have they ever asked me if I knew how to work on cars. They just assumed I did. I mean, I am a man, right? They began thanking me for stopping to help them before they even know if I can or not. Many women hate to admit it, but they have depended on men to help them, lead them, and protect them ever since creation. The women's lib crowd would never acknowledge it, but they do too. When their car breaks down, they don't go looking for long, legged blondes with fingernail polish and curly hair. They take their car to the men to repair. Men are the ones that can get it done. Chauvinistic? No. That is just life.

If something needs to be done, can you do it? Are you one of those men that people come to when they need something done? Or are you one of those men that have to go find another man to do it for you? Some men just have more gumption than others. There are men that can fix anything and do anything, and then there are those that can't do anything. What's the difference? The difference is gumption, or the lack of it. You see, every man has abilities. Some just haven't figured out what theirs are yet! They delight in saying "I can't..." or "I need..." They never stop to figure out a situation and make a clear, bold, workable plan to make it happen. They instead run for help or sit down and cry because they can't do it.

As a Dad, I do not permit my children to say "I can't." I rebuke them and lecture them every time they say that. I remind them that "I can't" never could! It may be difficult, and it may require some blood, sweat and tears, but "I can't" is not an excuse or a reason. I will sometimes give my sons a job to do just to test this very principle. I recently gave Spencer, who is eight years old, the job of filling the wheelbarrow with firewood and bringing it around to the side door. He ran and got the wheelbarrow and wheeled it around to the woodpile. He filled it to overflowing with logs. Then, he got mad because he couldn't push it. After a while, he looked me up, frustrated and worn out from trying to push that wheelbarrow full of logs. He said, "Daddy, I can't do it!" He was on the verge of tears at his feeble inabilities. What did I do? I know what a lot of parents would have done. They would have said, "Well, bless your heart, you tried. I'll handle it. You go play." Not me! I told him, "Yes, you can! I have never given you a job to do that you were not capable of doing. Now get around there and do what I told you to do." He got this look of complete defeat on his face and said, "Daddy, it's too heavy!" I asked him "Who's fault is that?" He looked at me and said, "Mine." I said, "You're exactly right. So why are you making that my problem?" He said, "I don't know." I told him that since he made it too heavy, that he could make it lighter. He finally caught on and went and took some of the wood off of the wheelbarrow and sure enough, he was able to complete the task.

Too many men are failing to recognize the fact that most of their problems are their own fault. If they never learn to fix their own mistakes and solve their own problems, they will never stop having problems. Part of being a man is having what it takes to diagnose the situation, mentally think through the problem and come up with a solution. That solution does not always include running for help. God gave you a brain and the capabilities to fix the problem yourself. Do you realize that Adam named every animal in the world all by himself? He didn't even have a dictionary or a thesaurus to consult! Do you realize that Noah and his three sons built an entire ark and rounded up two of every creature? Just the four of them? Was the task overwhelming? You bet! Was it possible? Apparently!

In Exodus chapter three and four, God gave Moses a task. That task involved going before Pharaoh and demanding that the nation of Israel be released from bondage. For two chapters, Moses made every excuse in the book for why he could not perform God's will. Interestingly enough, God didn't accept a single one of them. When God gives a man a job to do, He expects it to be done. Right. Now. A man with an "I can't" attitude will have a difficult time measuring up to the Biblical definitions of *The Exceptional Man*. A man who always begins his sentence with "I can't" is not a victor; he's a victim. And victims are losers.

Boldness of Enterprise

Gumption is an old Southern word that can be used in a variety of ways. There are a lot of men that lack their fair share of gumption. Boldness of enterprise is an interesting concept. In fact, the phrase almost smacks of irony. An enterprise is usually an intimidating venture. Embarking on a new enterprise many times comes with lot of gut-wrenching, hand-wringing and general uneasiness. Gumption is what a man needs to launch out into the deep. Gumption is that ability to stand up to seemingly overwhelming circumstances and not fall apart. Gumption is what enables a man to look danger, disappointment, failure and even death in the face without flinching.

Both as a businessman and as a Christian, gumption has been a defining element in my life. I am a dreamer. I am not content, however, to just dream. When I have an idea, I generally waste no time in trying to make that idea a reality. The difference in me and some men is we both have ideas, but some men never find out if theirs is great or not. They never do anything to make that dream come true.

In 1897, Henry Ford was excited about building the first, self-propelled carriage. He was so excited in fact that he built the car in his own garage. The only problem with that was there was no way to get it out! He had to break down a brick wall in his garage to get his car out and onto the street! While the rest of the world laughed at his idea of a horseless carriage, he boldly and eagerly proved them wrong.

The world also laughed at Thomas Edison and his light bulb theory. Robert Fulton's steamboat idea was not received too well. Samuel Morse proposed sending messages via wire and was rewarded with skepticism. Each of these men pursued their enterprises boldly and thankfully did not cave in to public opinion. The validity of an idea is not based on its reception; it is based on reality. The only way many times to know the reality of an idea's worth is to put it to the test – alone if need be.

The society we live in is so intrusive and outspoken that men today cannot think alone. They cannot think for themselves, and they cannot propel themselves. They must be pushed, coerced and even many times bribed just to perform their responsibilities. To find a man that has an idea and boldly pursues that idea under his own power is rare. I wonder how many men's inability to perform simple tasks in life has bled over into their spiritual life. They are always saying, "I can't!" and because they never try, they never do. Because their solution to the leaky toilet is "I can't," the toilet continues to leak. Because their answer to dealing with their pornography addiction is "I can't," the nightmare continues. They can't control their kids. They can't get their wife to follow. They can't witness to their peers. They can't pay their bills. They can't do anything they are supposed to do. Somewhere along the line, they adopted this helpless, weak, victim complex and then they wonder why they hate life.

Initiative

Initiative is a word you don't hear used often. It is even more rarely displayed. Initiative simply means *"the power or ability to begin or to follow through energetically with a plan or task; enterprise and determination."* Make no mistake about it – God calls men and God uses men that have initiative. Seeing something that needs doing and not attempting to do something about it is a disease among men today. It is this deficiency alone that is the reason for the utter complacency among our Christian men today. They do not take the initiative to change things. They see it happening, and they know there's a problem, but for them to actually roll up their sleeves and try and stop it is another story.

David was just a lowly shepherd boy. Possibly a teenager, but definitely a young man. He discovered Goliath screaming out profane blasphemies against his God and his country. For forty days, all the other soldiers had just stood there, trembling. No one even thought about accepting Goliath's challenge. David, on the other hand began to ask questions. "What shall be done to the man that killeth this Philistine, and taketh away the reproach from Israel? for who is this uncircumcised Philistine, that he should defy the armies of the living God?" (I Samuel 17:26) His brothers mistook his gumption for goading. "And Eliab his eldest brother heard when he spake unto the men; and Eliab's anger was kindled against David, and he said, Why camest thou down hither? and with whom hast thou left those few sheep in the wilderness? I know thy pride, and the naughtiness of thine heart; for thou art come down that thou mightest see the battle" (vs. 28). David was perplexed. Why weren't they doing something? Why was everybody just standing around? He defended his motives with this classic reply. "What have I now done? Is there not a cause?" Talk about initiative!

It never occurred to him that God would let him down. It never crossed his mind that he could lose. As John Maxwell so appropriately explained it, the soldiers saw this huge giant and didn't see how they could ever win. David saw Goliath and didn't see how he could miss! There was a job that needed to be done, and he did it. I wonder how many men we have in our churches today that even care enough to do something about the problems that plague our land. Abortion is legal, and the Christian men in this country do nothing. Same-sex marriage is constantly debated in the media, and the public never hear God's point of view. Where are the men? Where are those that see a problem and are willing to take action?

Aggressiveness and Guts

One of the most misunderstood qualities of a man is his God-given aggressiveness. "Blessed be the LORD my strength, which teacheth my hands to war, and my fingers to fight:" (Psalms 144:1) The opposite of aggressive is passive. Many men's defining characteristic would not be aggressive. They never attack anything. They are discouraged by the tall grass in the yard that needs to be cut. They moan and groan about the firewood that needs to be split. The car is just so dirty that they will never get it clean. The house needs painting, but it is just so big. Their teenagers are so rebellious that it's just no use to try and correct them. As the problems of life occur, passive men just sit and wring their hands. Men with gumption jump to their feet and attack the situation. They refuse to be beaten and overwhelmed. There has to be a way to do this!

Aggressive men are very intimidating creatures in today's society. Though women secretly admire strong, aggressive men, they many times deny it. The liberal feminists of our day have successfully brainwashed women into thinking that they don't need men for anything. Not even reproduction. Artificial insemination is becoming more and more popular, and men are just in the way and a nuisance. Many women treat aggressive men like rabid dogs that need to be caught and restricted and cured of their diseases. They openly decry the strong man's right to exist. They prefer the company of soft, weak men. Men they can control. Men they can train like lapdogs to respond to their every beck and call. Wimps.

Not only are strong men openly rebuked but secretly admired by many women, but also by many men. Aggressive men get elected into office by men that like what they see. They see the leadership qualities that are necessary to get a job done, and they cast their vote in favor of the man that they wish they could be. Aggressiveness is a quality that has been successfully squashed by a combination of domineering women and repeated failures. Show me a dominating wife, and I'll show you a husband that is weak. She would never admit he was weak, and neither would he. She would say he was sweet. She would say he was a gentleman. He would say the same thing, but let him stand up to her one time and see what happens.

"It is better to dwell in the corner of the housetop,
than with a brawling woman and in a wide house."
Proverbs 25:24

A dominating woman is the most vocal opponent to a man's natural aggression. She perceives his aggression as a threat to her right to rule. It startles her and makes her uneasy. She would loudly berate him for his failure to be the man she wants him to be, but the moment he started, she would yank him back into his proper place. She calls the shots. She gives the orders. She makes the decisions. She rules the roost. An aggressive man and a dominating woman cannot live under the same roof. "It is better to dwell in the wilderness, than with a contentious and an angry woman" (Proverbs 21:19). They will either kill one another, get a divorce, or one of them will have to submit to the other. Unfortunately, it is usually the man that cows down to the nagging wife. As time goes on, she drains every drop of aggression out of her man. The fiery, lively, fun-filled man she married slowly becomes her own little pre-programmed, lifeless failure. His aggression was too intimidating to her. It challenged her authority and her position in the home. The only time he gets aggressive is when he briefly defends his turf as the man of the house. He usually will blow off steam for a minute or two and then submit again. He will once again become the meek, quiet, discontented creature that she has so diligently manufactured.

Aggression is the gasoline that fuels the fires of success. Passive men are quitters. Passive men may have a vision, but they never see it fulfilled. I've seen house cats that were more aggressive than most men. If you invade their space, or rub them the wrong way, they just slither away and sit in the corner. They have no idea what it means to fight for what they believe in. They have no concept of defending truth and right. They have no desire to make anybody mad. They are so afraid of being perceived as mean or unkind. Their foremost desire is to live in peace and harmony with the world and to just live and let live. Living in peace is only possible if the righteous are in control, and passive men never control anything! Rather, they *are* controlled. "When the righteous are in authority, the people rejoice: but when the wicked beareth rule, the people mourn" (Proverbs 29:2).

I saw a bumper sticker some time ago that made a huge impression on me. It said, "God, Guns, and Guts made America great." I began to think about that statement. They have taken God out of the schools. They have tried to take Him out of everything actually. They are making new laws every year in their efforts to outlaw guns. Men have less guts and courage than they ever have before. What hope does America have to remain a great nation if the very elements that made her great are becoming extinct? What chance do our children have of growing up free if the men in our country no longer fight for what they believe in? As long as the men in this country are intimidated by atheists, the liberal media and bossy women, we have no hope of our boys ever seeing what a man really is.

A man was given dominion over creation in Genesis. Look around at what has happened. Men have been reduced to pawns and puppets. God give us some men with guts and a backbone that will stand up and take control of the situation. God give us men that will strap on their swords and fight for our families, our children and our faith. It is high time that Christian men get a burr under their saddle and kick out of the traces. It is time we make our voices heard and stop rolling over and playing dead. Get some fire in your bones and some grit in your craw and learn to take a stand! Rip off that muzzle and say something. Raise your voice and strengthen your hands for the fight. There's a job to do. If you won't do it, who will?

Too often the strong, silent man is silent only
because he does not know what to say,
and is reputed strong only because he has remained silent.
                        *- **Winston Churchill***

Chapter Six

The Exceptional Man's Goals

"I press toward the mark for the prize of the high calling of God in Christ Jesus."
(Philippians 3:14)

What are your goals? If you had to compile a list of your ambitions and your desires, could you do it? Many men today find themselves just living one day at a time. In essence, they are floating through life like a dead fish on a river. Whatever happens is fine with them. If something bad happens, they fuss and complain; and they get over it. If something good happens, they act like they won the lottery. One of the worst possible mindsets a man can have is the attitude that setting goals is pointless. An extremely harmful attitude among men is this "victim mentality." They feel that the whole world is out to get them. They feel that if they can just come home alive each night that they have survived. The highlight of the life of many men is the few minutes they spend in their recliner each night. When they grab that little black remote control, it is as if they are demonstrating the fact that they do indeed have some control over something! They guard that thing and fight over that thing because, for many men, the remote control is the only thing they actually have control over!

They don't like their job. They don't like their pay. They don't like their boss. They don't like the fact they are in debt. They don't like anything. The strange part is they do nothing to change their circumstances! Whose life is it anyway? Who made them get a job there? Who made them settle for those wages? Who made them buy all that stuff on credit? They come home from work every day disgusted with life, disgusted with themselves and everybody around them. What happened to the concept of "just whistle while you work"? What happened to the illusions of coming home from work and grabbing a quick shower and playing in the floor with the kids? What happened to walking in the door and grabbing the wife around the waist and kissing her passionately? I'll tell you what happened. Somewhere, that man failed to set some goals in his life. He just lived one day at a time, and now he's tired and frustrated and broke, and he swears it's not his fault! I can assure you of one thing: either you will spend your life fulfilling your own dreams or the dreams of someone else. The choice is up to you. Men were meant to dream. They were designed to have plans and achieve them. What is so sad is that many men never realize that dreams really can come true.

The Plague of Apathy

One of my favorite topics is the subject of ambition. It is so hard to find a man these days that has any zeal, any ambition, and any fervency at all. If there is a word that describes men today, it would have to be "apathy." They just don't care. If you can ever get them motivated, you can't keep them motivated! They are like so many children. They get excited about something, and then lose interest after about ten minutes. If it is difficult, if it requires some of their free time, or if it costs them anything, they're not interested. How else would you explain why men can drive cars for years that leak oil all over the driveway? How else would you explain why a toilet can leak, and they just shove a bucket under it and forget about it? What would compel a man to walk through the house with mud on his boots after his wife has spent all day cleaning? I tell you what it is. Apathy! They just don't care.

This attitude of apathy cannot be confused with laziness. Laziness is one thing. Apathy is another. That same man that drives the car with an oil leak most likely works on cars all day. And mind you, he works hard! But when it comes time to work on his own car, he just doesn't care enough about it to fix it. That man that tracks mud through the house probably worked like a dog all day and just didn't feel like taking his boots off at the door. These silly examples of apathy reflect something that goes much deeper than the oil that is dripping on the driveway. It goes a lot deeper than the mud on the carpet. An attitude of apathy is one of the worst problems that could plague a man. It defines a man's very existence and paves the way for his future.

Let me make another point on this subject of apathy. Apathy is not ignorance. Many men know what they should do, and they know how to do it. The problem is not that they are stupid; the problem is they are not concerned enough about it to change. Some men enjoy the "security" of that very job that they hate. If they woke up and discovered that they had been fired or laid off, they would rush back to that very job they despise and to that very boss they hate and beg for their job back! Their security is more important to them than being happy. They would rather let others make the decisions and determine their fate in life than to actually climb in the driver's seat and steer their own destiny.

Taking Control of Your Life

Let's get one thing established. Unless you are chained in a dungeon somewhere or are locked up in a jailhouse, you have control over your life. What you do with it is up to you. When you die, the legacy you leave behind will be entirely your choice. If you don't believe that, then you are inflicted with a "victim mentality!" Nobody has ever looked down into a coffin and said, "Poor guy, he could have been somebody, but people just wouldn't let him!" Anybody that has ever become somebody had to do it in spite of everybody! Every man throughout history that has ever been successful did it on purpose. Another common characteristic of successful men has been their willingness to accept the blame for their failures. Failures do not become successful by blaming everybody else for their failures. Persistence is invaluable, and so is accountability. People hate to hear losers saying, "I couldn't help it!"

When it comes to a man's spiritual temperature, his personal qualities definitely come into play. A lazy man will not be a spiritual man because he won't put forth the effort. An apathetic man will never be spiritual because it is not a priority. A negative man will not be spiritual because it is not possible. A quitter will not be a spiritual man because it's just too difficult. A man's character will be a huge factor in his walk with God. We have a desperate need for men that walk with God, but it does not happen by chance. It is not a pill you buy at the store. It is a daily pursuing of God's will and God's plan for your life.

What are your goals in life? If you do not have any goals in your daily life, more than likely you do not have any in your spiritual life. Men that cry about being a victim of circumstance in their finances or in their work will do the same when it comes to their spiritual life. A man with an "I can't help it" attitude will find himself getting frustrated when it comes to living up to God's expectations of a Christian. Until he is willing to grab the bull by the horns, stand up, make a decision to be somebody for God and put forth the effort to do it, it simply will not happen! Serving God is a decision. It is also a lifestyle. It requires determination, but in order to be determined, you must have something to strive for. Unless you have goals that are defined, you will never achieve those goals.

Looking back on my life as a Christian, I have read numerous biographies of great Christians. I have read of their successes and failures. I learned how they overcame the obstacles in their life. I became inspired by the fact that in their generation, they stood head and shoulders above the others, simply because they had a desire. It was not a desire to look good or impress people. It was a desire to make a difference in the life of someone else. It was a burning desire to make their life count. Men are not born great. They are born just like everybody else. The difference in great men and average men is the ambition and the effort they put forth to achieve that goal. As someone once said, the difference in the ordinary and the extraordinary is that little extra effort!

Just Keep On!

When you feel that you have fought as long as you can fight,
And that Satan has attacked you with all his force and might.
When daybreak is slow arriving and you are hindered by the night,
When it seems that there's no possible way you'll ever escape your plight –
Just keep on!

When the storm clouds gather thick and there's darkness all around,
When it seems that all your brethren are trying to pull you down,
When you pray to God above and in return you hear no sound,
When the forces of "ole" Satan continue to abound –
Just keep on!

*When a load of doubt and despair you've been allowed to carry
And you're beaten down by storm after storm of Satan's wrath and fury,
When your moods of despair and happiness seem to fluctuate and vary
When under the pressures of life you feel you're just about to be buried –
Just keep on!*

*When your friends and family forsake you and leave you all alone
When you get down on your knees to pray and all you can do is groan
When your warnings of love and compassion seem to fall on hearts of stone
When your body is tired and weary from trying to make Jesus known –
Just keep on!*

By M. S. Shiflett

What are Your Plans?

Amazingly enough, the only goals that some men set are strictly financial. They put money aside, make investments, start a retirement fund, or make a series of financial decisions. Their goal is to be financially secure or independent or to simply have enough to retire on and live out their life comfortably. Other than that, they really give no thought to their future. They fail to realize that life is a path. Every day is a step in any given direction. They do not stop to think about where their life is headed. If they would only hesitate and ask themselves the question, "If I keep on going in the direction I'm going, where will I end up?" then they would no doubt give more serious thought to the path they are on.

Where are you headed? What is your purpose in life? Is it to just survive the daily grind? Is it to keep your head above water? Or do you have a workable plan in mind of becoming a man that God would be pleased with? When I speak of God being pleased, I'm not talking about Him being pleased with you on a daily level. I'm talking about your life as a whole. Notice what Paul said at the end of his life in II Timothy 4:7: "I have fought a good fight, I have finished my course, I have kept the faith:" What a testimony! Paul's life was a success because he stayed on course. One of the most motivating forces in my life is the prospect of hearing the Lord say to me one day, "Well done, good and faithful servant; thou hast been faithful over a few things, I will make thee ruler over many things: enter thou into the joy of thy lord" (Matthew 25:23).

In Paul's life, he defined his goals in several places. Paul was a man that was driven. Every waking moment was one continuous effort to fulfil his ambition. He was constantly working to fulfil the call of God for his life. In all actuality, apart from God's call, he had no life! His entire life was totally consumed with doing what God had called him to do. To Paul, the ministry was more than an occupation; it was an obsession. He was consumed with the ministry. In spite of all of his achievements and his ministry, he had set some goals in his life on a more spiritual level. In Philippians 3:10-14, we find a list of objectives that Paul relayed to the church at Philippi detailing his desire to grow closer to God and be more effective as a man. Notice the chart below to understand the goals that Paul set in his personal life and what it would take to accomplish those goals. Setting goals without understanding what it would take to achieve those goals are a complete waste of time.

Paul's Goal	**Bible Verse**	**Requirement**
Familiarity	that I may know him	Study
Force	the power of his resurrection	Spirit-filling
Fellowship	the fellowship of his sufferings	Suffering
Fashioning	made conformable to his death	Submission
Focus	forgetting those things	Surrender
Fulfillment	reaching forth unto those things	Stamina

The Proper Perspective on Riches

There is an unprecedented emphasis in the past few years on the importance of prosperity. Preachers and bookstores are filled with unscriptural admonitions concerning God's desire for you to be wealthy. The Bible is filled with verses that describe God's definition of prosperity. Contrary to what some people say, God is far more concerned about your spiritual prosperity than He is your financial prosperity. Over and over again, God's word reminds us of the vanity and foolishness of material wealth. Notice just a few of God's exhortations concerning the proper attitude toward riches.

God rewarded Solomon with unbelievable wealth simply for having the proper perspective on life. "And God said unto him, Because thou hast asked this thing, and hast not asked for thyself long life; neither hast asked riches for thyself, nor hast asked the life of thine enemies; but hast asked for thyself understanding to discern judgment." (1 Kings 3:11).

Solomon went on to later write that "He that trusteth in his riches shall fall: but the righteous shall flourish as a branch" (Proverbs 11:28). "There is that maketh himself rich, yet hath nothing: there is that maketh himself poor, yet hath great riches" (Proverbs 13:7). He understood that having money does not make a man rich!

"A good name is rather to be chosen than great riches, and loving favour rather than silver and gold" (Proverbs 22:1). Are you more concerned about your name and your testimony than about your bank account? Which one is more important to you?

"Wilt thou set thine eyes upon that which is not? for riches certainly make themselves wings; they fly away as an eagle toward heaven" (Proverbs 23:5). Riches are temporary, and wealth is a lingering mist. "For riches are not for ever: and doth the crown endure to every generation?" (Proverbs 27:24).

The greatest bit of wisdom that can be found in this realm of wealth is having the desire for basic necessities. Solomon prayed, "Remove far from me vanity and lies: give me neither poverty nor riches; feed me with food convenient for me:" (Proverbs 30:8). Jesus preached more about money than probably any other man. His advice to men everywhere was very simple. In Matthew 6:24, Jesus clearly taught that "No man can serve two masters: for either he will hate the one, and love the other; or else he will hold to the one, and despise the other. Ye cannot serve God and mammon (wealth)." He went on to preach, "But seek ye first the kingdom of God, and his righteousness; and all these things shall be added unto you." What "things" was He referring to? Wealth and riches? No! He was referring to food and clothing! Basis necessities is all God has promised us. He has not promised us riches down here. We will all experience untold wealth one day in Heaven. That is good enough for me!

If we could get men today to put forth as much effort to seek the furtherance of the kingdom of God as they do to seek the furtherance of their wealth, we could revolutionize the world. Men are filled with schemes and plans to increase their riches, while the work of God and the church is floundering. The best advice I can find on this subject of accumulating material wealth is found in Matthew 6:19-21. "Lay not up for yourselves treasures upon earth, where moth and rust doth corrupt, and where thieves break through and steal: But lay up for yourselves treasures in heaven, where neither moth nor rust doth corrupt, and where thieves do not break through nor steal: For where your treasure is, there will your heart be also."

Who Are You Trying to Please?

I am in awe many times at men. They may be intelligent and impressive, but they are afraid of what people think of them. Their main objective in life is to make somebody else happy. We're talking about goals here. We're talking about setting goals and achieving them. I can tell you right now, if your goal is to please somebody else, your goals are out of line. I know some men that try the impossible: they try to please everybody. If you live your life trying to please others, you will not please yourself, and you will definitely not please God. If you're trying to please God, you will surely not please others. If you are trying to please others, you will not please God. "For do I now persuade men, or God? or do I seek to please men? for if I yet pleased men, I should not be the servant of Christ" (Galatians 1:10).

People are cruel. First of all, they will not define their expectations. You can work day and night for fifty years and not please those around you. Secondly, people's expectations change. They think you should be doing this, and about the time you accomplish it, they've changed their mind and you're back to square one. Trying to please people is like a dog chasing its tail. You'll be running in circles, exerting all your energy for something that is impossible to accomplish.

You must not allow others to define your goals. If it is not your goal, it is not going to happen – no matter how worthy the cause. How far will you go to please somebody? Will you take a job you do not like? Will you spend time doing something you do not care about? Will you let others dictate your schedule, your routine, your plans and your life just to have their acceptance?

Some men resemble a dog. A dog will jump in ice cold water to fetch a stick, swim all the way back and drop it at his master's feet just for a pat on the head and a "Good boy!"

Some men will do anything for a little love and recognition from somebody they admire. If all you ever do in life is run in circles to have the approval of man, you will look back over your life one day and hate yourself for being such an idiot. You might have been doing the right things, but you weren't doing them for the right reasons, and therefore there was no fulfillment in them. "Not with eyeservice, as menpleasers; but as the servants of Christ, doing the will of God from the heart;" (Ephesians 6:6).

There is no satisfaction in trying to please men. It is frustrating, it is aggravating and it is impossible. People will use you and abuse you to promote their own goals and ambitions. If you are not careful, you will find yourself being the loser. While you were being used to fulfil somebody else's dream, you never fulfiled yours. Do not misunderstand my point. I fully comprehend the Biblical role of being a servant and bearing one another's burdens. I am not denying the fact that we are to help one another and support one another and do everything we can to help our brothers and sisters in the Lord. I am not talking about serving. I am talking about living your life to try and please others. God even commands the employees to do what they do to please God, not their employer. "Servants, obey in all things your masters according to the flesh; not with eyeservice, as menpleasers; but in singleness of heart, fearing God:" (Colossians 3:22). If what you do is not pleasing God, it is a waste of time! Don't do it! Find out what God's will is for your life and get busy doing it. If God's will is for you to be in a supportive role as a second man, then tackle it with gusto and God will bless you.

Are You For Real?

In this matter of setting goals and pleasing God, sincerity is a must. If what you are doing is all about putting on a show, you can forget it! Not only will people see right through it, but God will not accept it. Many men, in their attempt to just get people off of their backs, play a game. Maybe their wife is nagging them to be more involved in the church, or their pastor is nailing them from the pulpit for their lack of faithfulness. In their efforts to get some relief, they will commit to something they are not sincere about. They might even undertake a ministry position or volunteer for some outreach that they quite frankly could not care less about. They think if they portray an image of being spiritual, it will make them spiritual. Nothing could be further from the truth. "Having a form of godliness, but denying the power thereof: from such turn away" (2 Timothy 3:5). Paul commanded Timothy to avoid hypocrites; men that had a form of godliness, but no power to accompany it.

If you do what you do just to get somebody "off of your back," then you are guilty of being a man-pleaser. If you are blessed enough to have somebody in your life encouraging you to do more for God, then praise the Lord for that. Everybody needs a cheerleader and a motivator at times to help keep them on the right track. But if for some reason you have no desire to do anything for God, yet you try to make people think you do, you are being a hypocrite and a deceiver. The solution is not to tackle a job or a ministry or a task just because somebody is asking you to. What you need to do is find out why you do not want to do it, and start from there. Is it because of laziness? Is it because there is no vision? Is it because you do not feel worthy to do something of that magnitude? Could it be that you are too selfish with your own time and resources to "waste" it doing other things? Until you diagnose the problem, you cannot properly solve it. Faking spirituality is definitely not the answer.

I am convinced that many men today that are in a leadership position are guilty of leading a double life. They allowed themselves to get caught up in a job and they felt too guilty for not wanting to do it that they just played along. Now, they are in a position of leadership and their heart is not sincere, their heart is not in it and they are in too deep to get out. In their efforts to impress others, they allowed themselves to get sucked up in a whirlpool of deceit, frustration and helplessness. It is very clear from Scripture that many religious leaders are not even born again! Notice the words of Jesus Christ when he addressed the disciples. "Many will say to me in that day, Lord, Lord, have we not prophesied in thy name? and in thy name have cast out devils? and in thy name done many wonderful works? And then will I profess unto them, I never knew you: depart from me, ye that work iniquity" (Matthew 7:22, 23).

How do you explain these verses? Jesus said there would be many! Preachers, evangelists, missionaries, and ministers of every description will be standing before God having spent their lives in vain. For some reason, they got involved in the ministry and were not even born again! Maybe they thought it was an honorable endeavor. They might have had friends that talked them into it. Some of these preachers may have been "mamma called and daddy sent." Whatever the reason, they were fakes. All of them. Jesus will look at them and say, "I never knew you!" What a shock that will be to them. What an even greater shock it will be to their followers. What about you? Are you real?

In a man's life, there will come a time when he must sit down and define his future. He must decide what God's will is for him and make an honest effort to accomplish that will. Those goals may not be easy, and they may not be popular. It might not include getting rich or becoming famous. That doesn't matter. God expects men to have some purpose in life, and in order to have a purpose, you need to know who you are, why you are here, and what you are supposed to be doing. Define your goals. In spite of all the opposition that you will encounter, you have a job to do. Understand God's expectations of you as a man and get busy!

Chapter Seven

The Exceptional Man's Guidance

"A good man sheweth favour, and lendeth: he will guide his affairs with discretion."
(Psalms 112:5)

  To live in a world where women are seeking and achieving male domination is very depressing for the Christian man. For women to seek equality and fair treatment is one thing, and quite understandable. Their desire to rule the world is both unscriptural and unimaginable. God very clearly laid out man's responsibilities and his job description just before creating him from the dust of the ground. "And God said, <u>Let us make man in our image</u>, after our likeness: <u>and let them have dominion</u> over the fish of the sea, and over the fowl of the air, and over the cattle, and <u>over all the earth</u>, and over every creeping thing that creepeth upon the earth" Genesis 1:26.

  Later on, we find God created Eve to be Adam's help meet. She was created to help him fulfil his duty of having dominion over the earth. I am not going to elaborate on the role of women according to God's word, but I do want to stress a point. It appears that the time has come when men are content to sit back and let the women not only lead in the workplace and in government, but also in the work of God. Where are the MEN today that will stand up and fulfil their God-given responsibilities? Where are the MEN today that will go the extra mile to see that God's work is accomplished?

Curses and Chores

Even as a young man, I was both amused and astounded at women's stubborn insistence at being on the blunt end of both curses: hers and the man's. In Genesis 3:16, God clearly told the woman that her curse was to have pain in childbearing. He also told her "and thy desire shall be to thy husband, and he shall rule over thee." This was her curse for listening to the advice of the serpent, Satan himself. She failed to heed the warnings of her husband, and she succumbed to her desire to eat the forbidden fruit. In doing so, she plunged all of humanity into a sinful state. God's punishment was not hers only, but for all the women that would follow her down through time. There is no Biblical record of this curse ever being revoked.

On the other hand, the man's curse was also quite severe – considering how good he had it up until now. God said to Adam, "... Because thou hast hearkened unto the voice of thy wife, and hast eaten of the tree, of which I commanded thee, saying, Thou shalt not eat of it: cursed is the ground for thy sake; in sorrow shalt thou eat of it all the days of thy life; Thorns also and thistles shall it bring forth to thee; and thou shalt eat the herb of the field; In the sweat of thy face shalt thou eat bread, till thou return unto the ground; for out of it wast thou taken: for dust thou art, and unto dust shalt thou return" (Genesis 3:17-19).

The man's curse was that he had to contend with a cursed ground, thorns, thistles and work for his daily bread until the day he died. Why was he cursed? According to God, it was "Because thou hast hearkened unto the voice of thy wife. . . ."

God cursed Adam with a very severe curse because he failed to exercise his God-given authority over his wife. He allowed her to lead him, and the results were disastrous. From that day until just a few decades ago, the women were content to allow the man to bear his curse and they bore their own. His curse was working for the food and hers was pain in childbearing and submitting to her husband. In case this does not set well with the women folk, and they plead "Old Testament law," let me remind you that there is a huge difference in a law and a curse. This wasn't a law that was done away with in the New Testament. Actually, these two curses are the basis for many New Testament passages. We will look at many of them as we progress through this book. However, let's take the time to examine another portion of Scripture that reiterates what these verses teach.

In Titus chapter two, Paul commanded Titus, a young pastor, to convey to his people some basic rules of Christianity. One of them is the fact that the wife is supposed to be a keeper at home. Notice with me the wording of this Scripture. "That they may teach the young women to be sober, to love their husbands, to love their children, To be discreet, chaste, keepers at home, good, obedient to their own husbands, that the word of God be not blasphemed" (Titus 2:4, 5). Now why would a woman insist on being saddled with her curse and her husband's when she has a Biblical right to only have to deal with one?

What was God's directive to the New Testament Christian man? I Timothy 5:8 says, "But if any provide not for his own, and specially for those of his own house, he hath denied the faith, and is worse than an infidel." It is very obvious that the man of the house was responsible for providing for the family. If there is no husband, that would be an entirely different scenario. What is my point? My point is very simple – if you are a man, you need to find a job. It is your responsibility according to the word of God.

Who is in Charge?

We need to establish a very crucial Biblical fact concerning leadership. In spite of what anybody says, the word of God, the Final Authority for all matters of faith and practice is very clear, and the verdict stands. God NEVER intended for women to lead. That responsibility was given to the men. One of God's expectations of manhood is that each and every man be able to lead and guide those under him and around him in the paths of righteousness. Call me old fashioned, call me chauvinistic. I do not mind because I have studied my Bible. God's word is very clear that the wife is supposed to follow her husband. Men are to lead the home. "Wives, submit yourselves unto your own husbands, as unto the Lord" (Ephesians 5:22). It is also explained again in 1 Peter 3:1, "Likewise, ye wives, be in subjection to your own husbands; that, if any obey not the word, they also may without the word be won by the conversation of the wives."

How anybody could possibly misunderstand the spiritual leadership role of the husband is beyond me. Beginning in the Garden of Eden, God relayed the instruction concerning the tree of knowledge of good and evil prior to Eve's creation. It was Adam's responsibility to inform the woman of God's instruction. This example is given when Paul instructed Timothy to "Let the woman learn in silence with all subjection. But I suffer not a woman to teach, nor to usurp authority over the man, but to be in silence. For Adam was first formed, then Eve" (I Timothy 2:11-13). People can try and explain that portion of scripture away all they want to, but it doesn't change the meaning. As an intelligent man with excellent reading and comprehension skills, I do not need a feminist trying to tell me what those verses are talking about. God clearly forbids women from having authority over a man. He even forbad them to teach men.

Before we can examine the details of man's leadership, we must determine man's duty to lead. God placed the husband over the wife in the home, and he placed men in the leadership positions of the church. The requirements and qualifications for a bishop were very clearly directed toward men. Notice these verses that explain God's plan concerning the church leaders. I Timothy 3:1 states, "This is a true saying, If a <u>man</u> desire the office of a bishop, he desireth a good work." Further down, it elaborates. "A bishop then must be blameless, <u>the husband of one wife</u> . . . ." It is explained even better in verses 4 and 5, "One that ruleth well his own house, having his children in subjection with all gravity; (For if a man know not how to rule his own house, how shall he take care of the church of God?)" How can a woman hold the office of bishop, pastor, elder, etc. if the qualification is to be the husband of one wife? How can a woman be a husband? How can a woman rule her house if the ruler of the house is supposed to be a man according to Ephesians 5:22-24? "Wives, submit yourselves unto your own husbands, as unto the Lord. For the husband is the head of the wife, even as Christ is the head of the church: and he is the saviour of the body. Therefore as the church is subject unto Christ, so let the wives be to their own husbands in every thing." It is logically impossible and it is scripturally impossible for a woman to rule a church.

The problem with Christianity today is that there is a vast shortage of MEN that are willing to lead. You can walk into most churches today and there are more women and children than men. Because men down through the years have neglected their God-given responsibility to lead, women have been left with the burden. Many women do not want to be the leader. They resent their husbands for not shouldering his responsibility, and they get bitter in their hearts because of it. In turn, they nag and whine and rebuke their husbands. God's will for the men is for them to be the spiritual leaders in the home and in the church.

God clearly forbade the women from holding a position of authority over men. Today, we have women in leadership positions that God never intended. I have just one profound fact to present. It is impossible for a woman to be a man of God! The phrase "man of God" is found in the King James Bible a total of 73 times; "woman of God" is never found. A woman that usurps authority over a man is doing so against the clear teachings of the Scripture. A woman in charge has perverted God's role for the family and has placed the husband in a position as helpmeet. That is her job! As men, we need to resume our positions as the leaders. It is time for us to put our pants on and take over the job of guiding our wives and our children. We have neglected our responsibilities long enough!

Character

An alarming trend has become evident in recent years. Character and integrity are being mocked as old fashioned and outdated. Anybody that holds to principles are laughed at and derided. An excellent example of this trend was the public reaction to the Clinton-Lewinsky scandal. The fact that the President lied under oath, not to mention cheated on his wife, seemed to have little or no bearing on people's perception of him. When the news came out, I distinctly remember talking with a young man that was a freshman in college. He insisted that the President's character was completely irrelevant to his being qualified to lead our country. I was appalled to hear that intelligence, ability, popularity and prestige made integrity obsolete! Many people feel that way today. Fortunately, we have an unwavering authority on the subject to which we can refer for times like these. The word of God gives more than adequate instruction as to the importance of character and the fact that it plays a direct part in a man's ability to lead.

Joseph is an excellent example of a young man with unquestionable character. He had many opportunities to make wrong decisions but always did what was right. In Genesis 37, we find the character of Joseph evident even at the early age of 17. He brought to his father the evil report of his brethren. Instead of getting involved in whatever it was they were doing, he left and told his father. His father trusted him and loved him more than all of the other sons. This love was manifested by his gift of a coat of many colors. Because of Joseph's character and his dreams, his brethren schemed and plotted to destroy him. At the last moment, Joseph was sold into slavery. After arriving in Egypt, he became the slave of Potiphar, the captain of the guard. Again, his character set the stage for a promotion, and Potiphar made Joseph the overseer of his house.

Soon after Joseph's promotion, his master's wife began to try and seduce him. We do not know how long he resisted her advances, but the fact that he did it at all speaks highly of his character. Most men in his position would have given in. Many men would have been seducing her before she had a chance to do so herself! Not Joseph. The Bible says "Joseph was a goodly person, and well favoured." When she daily harassed him to lie with her, Joseph's answer was a classic. His reply was ". . . how can I do this great wickedness, and sin against God?" His fleeing her proposals cost him his freedom, but it didn't cost him his integrity. Your character and your integrity are something that nobody can take away from you. It is you that offers it up on the altar of self-gratification. Joseph's character made him a man of principle later on when he became the prime minister of Egypt. Did Joseph have a victim mentality? Not on your life! He was an overcomer – in spite of his family, his friends and even his flesh.

What about Daniel? As a young man, Daniel had been kidnapped and taken to a strange land. In this land were strange people, strange practices and strange gods. In Daniel chapter 1, we find Daniel and his friends chosen by the king because of their extraordinary abilities. The Bible describes them as "Children in whom was no blemish, but well favoured, and skilful in all wisdom, and cunning in knowledge, and understanding science, and such as had ability in them to stand in the king's palace. . . ." (Daniel 1:4). These were not just a bunch of pimply-faced teenagers. They were extremely intelligent, very attractive young men with a great personality, skill and ability. They were placed in a large group made up of other young men of equal abilities. However, in verse four, Daniel exemplifies something greater than looks, intelligence or ability. He demonstrated his character. The Bible says that he "purposed in his heart not to defile himself with a portion of the king's meat."

Being a man with an abnormal IQ, no doubt Daniel fully realized the possibilities of this commitment. Even after being confronted with the possibility of his decision costing the prince of the eunuchs his head, Daniel refused to back down. His mind was made up. His principles took precedence over position, popularity, prestige or payment. Daniel's character proved to be his greatest asset later on. Like Joseph, Daniel was placed second in command in chapter two verse 48. Rest assured – character is a must! Not only must a man have unquestionable character, he must also possess unshakeable convictions.

Convictions

What motivates you? Fear of man? Lust for money? The promise of fame? If these are your key motivators, you will not be a man of conviction. A man of conviction is a man that will do what he believes is right, no matter what anybody else says. He is not intimidated by intellects. He is not bothered by bullies. He is not afraid of attacks. He will not be hindered by haughty opposition. A man of conviction will keep on keeping on, no matter what it costs him. Are you a man of conviction?

There is a thin line between conviction and stubborn hard-headedness. Some men are stubborn, but they are not men of conviction. I am not referring to your dogmatic refusal to pick your dirty clothes up from off the floor! Convictions are personal abiding persuasions that will dictate your course in life. A man without convictions and principles is like a ship without a rudder. There is nothing to dictate your direction but the opinions of the people around you. A man without convictions will wet his finger and test the wind before making a decision. Polls, surveys and people's opinions are poor substitutes for principles. If you examine the crossroad ahead and choose the smoother of the two, you may find yourself on a smooth ride to nowhere. Taking the road less traveled is one common characteristic of great men. Convictions and principles are what keep men on the road to greatness. Whatever you do, never mistake popularity or being famous for true greatness. God is the ultimate judge of who is great and who is not.

Whether you are a pastor with a church to lead or a teenager in high school, you must have some convictions in your life, or it will be a life of complete instability. David put it this way in Psalms 4:26, 27: "Ponder the path of thy feet, and let all thy ways be established. Turn not to the right hand nor to the left: remove thy foot from evil." There are a lot of men today that are turning to the right or the left. They cannot seem to get on the right track and stay on it. They listen to everybody else and they cannot make up their mind what they want to do. In another place, David gave his testimony. He stressed the fact that he knew where he was going and why. "He brought me up also out of an horrible pit, out of the miry clay, and set my feet upon a rock, and established my goings" (Psalms 40:2).

James put it this way. "A double minded man is unstable in all his ways" (James 1:8). We all know men that cannot seem to find their way. It is because somewhere along the way, they ditched principle and conviction for something of less value. Some men exchange principle for popularity. Men of principle are, many times, lonely men. They do not find the masses crowding around them because the masses like people that cater to their whims and wants. As I said earlier, just because a man is popular doesn't make him a man of principle. On the other hand, just because a man is hated doesn't make him a man of principle either. Principles are only as good as their foundation. If your principles and convictions are based on your logic, your upbringing, your education, your environment or something else, don't bank on them being right. The best principles to have are those based on the authority of God's word. No matter what comes your way, godly principles and convictions will see you through the storm and give you peace in your heart and mind. Convictions will produce confidence. Convictions will also produce consistency.

A certain amount of opposition is a great help to a man; it is what he wants and must have to be good for anything. Hardship and opposition are the native soil of manhood and self-reliance.
- John Neal

Having a basic understanding of right and wrong is a good start, but is not going to produce convictions in your life. Being convinced that you are on the right path will require a deeper understanding of God's word. Some men may think they have convictions, but they really only have preferences. They prefer one road over another, but if push comes to shove, they will change roads every time. That is not conviction. A man of conviction will stay on the right road, even if he has to crawl over logs, rocks, roadblocks and potholes.
There is nothing that can sway a man of principle. In years gone by, millions of Christians were martyred for their faith in Jesus Christ. They were burned at the stake, stoned, sawed in half and suffered many other unspeakable atrocities. Why?

They believed in something. That something they believed in was worth dying for. No amount of pressure, problems or persecution could cause them to deviate from the course they had chosen. Are you a man of conviction? What does it take to change your mind? Can you stand alone?

Compassion

A man in a leadership position must have compassion. Compassion is perceived by some men to be a sign of weakness. That is not true. Compassion is a vital element in the life of any leader. Whether it is a husband, a father, a teacher or a pastor, a healthy dose of compassion is a necessity. Jesus was the greatest example of a compassionate leader. "But when he saw the multitudes, he was moved with compassion on them, because they fainted, and were scattered abroad, as sheep having no shepherd" (Matthew 9:36). His heart was constantly affected by what He saw and the needs of the people that looked up to Him. As we've already seen, Jesus was anything but weak. His love for people and for the work was a huge motivation for Him. Compassion is not just an abstract expression. Compassion is very real and very powerful. Jude reminds us that with compassion, we can increase our impact on those around us. "And of some have compassion, making a difference:" (Jude 1:22). If you want to make a difference in the lives of those around you, you must exemplify Christ-like compassion and empathy for them.

Compassion is a combination of love and being able to relate to the needs of others. We easily imagine having compassion for a puppy with a hurt paw or a child with a physical problem. But sometimes, compassion is needed with people with no obvious problem. People have needs, fears, and weaknesses. If the leader in their life doesn't love them for who they are, they will never receive the help and direction that they need. Compassion is a very self-less attribute. It means putting yourself and your needs aside in order to focus on somebody else. It is not always reciprocated, or even appreciated, as with the case of Jesus and the nation of Israel. Sometimes no matter how much you love those you are leading, it will not change the way they look at you. That is an unfortunate fact. Normally, people that do not recognize compassion are usually very hard and cold themselves. Whether your concern for people is realized or not, it is an extremely vital element in leadership. A leader without compassion becomes a dictator and a tyrant. If you want to be the kind of man that Jesus was, you must find room in your heart for compassion towards people and their needs.

Sometimes, it is difficult to relate to people and their needs. This has been one of the most challenging areas of ministry for me. I find it hard sometimes to relate to people who lived a life filled with gross immorality, drunkenness, drugs and other sins. I grew up in a Christian home and was born again at the tender age of four. My dad was a pastor and a missionary. My whole life was centered around the Lord, church and the Bible. Now that I am in the ministry, I find it difficult to relate to people that came from a life of sin. Sometimes instead of compassion, I only feel contempt. Sometimes it is hard to have compassion for people that have gotten themselves in a mess. In spite of my flesh, I do my best to reach out to them. Many times my efforts are ignored because they do not think I care. I do care, even though I never experienced it myself. Jesus never experienced being demon possessed, but he still cared for those that were. Jesus never committed adultery, but he showed compassion to the woman at the well in John chapter four. Experience is not always necessary to show compassion. Likewise, experience is not always a guarantee that you will show compassion. Compassion is a heart and mind condition. If your heart is right and your mind is right, you will find that it is easier to love those in need.

Control

A vital element to leadership is the ability to control. Not others, but yourself. There are so many men that think that controlling and dominating people are the trademarks of a great leader. That is so untrue. A great leader will first learn to control himself, and then he can learn to control others. The Bible speaks of men that are "incontinent" in II Timothy chapter three. The word means "lack of self control; intemperate." The sin of incontinence is one that is many times ignored and mislabeled as personality or style. A man that is unable to control himself is a bad leader. There are several elements of control that a man should learn to exhibit if he wants to be a successful guide. He must first learn to control his mind. Much could be said about mind control, but Satan's greatest area of attack is in a man's mind. What we think – we do. Proverbs 23:7 says, "For as he thinketh in his heart, so is he. . . ." Controlling one's mind hinges greatly on what goes into the mind. It would be safe to say that a man that has been watching lewd, sensual shows on television will battle lewd, sensual thoughts for the rest of the day. Reading books, magazines or periodicals that focus on negativism would definitely have a bearing on a man's thought pattern.

God understands the human mind far greater than anyone else. That is why God very clearly prescribes what should dominate our thoughts. The Psalmist David understood the impact a man's mind plays on his entire life. He put it this way, "But his delight is in the law of the LORD and in his law doeth he meditate day and night" (Psalms 1:2). The previous verse details the blessed man's walk, company and daily lifestyle. Verse two explains that a man that loves and meditates on the word of God will live a godly life – no matter what is going on around him. I am convinced that most of the inner sins are a direct result of one's thought life. Covetousness, bitterness, envy, jealousy and anger are all the product of meditating on the wrong things. Men covet because they think about what they have or don't have. Men become angry because they did not mentally prepare themselves to be violated or disappointed. Men become jealous because they think they are inadequate or inferior to another person. Many other sins are because of a carnal thought life. Jesus explained it by saying, "But I say unto you, That whosoever looketh on a woman to lust after her hath committed adultery with her already in his heart" (Matthew 5:28). Adultery is not a sin that men fall into. They think about it, scheme, plan, devise and when all the pieces are in place, they walk into it with their eyes wide open. The thoughts of man dictate the actions of man. If you can not control your mind, you will never be much in the way of a godly man.

What about your tongue? Can you control your tongue? It is obvious from Scripture that any man that can control his tongue is a mature man. "For in many things we offend all. If any man offend not in word, the same is a perfect man, and able also to bridle the whole body" (James 3:2). A man that can learn when to speak and when to remain silent is worth his weight in gold. The Bible is filled with admonitions concerning the tongue and its role in our everyday lives. A man's tongue is the faucet from which the waters of the soul flow. Jesus worded it like this, "A good man out of the good treasure of his heart bringeth forth that which is good; and an evil man out of the evil treasure of his heart bringeth forth that which is evil: for of the abundance of the heart his mouth speaketh" (Luke 6:45). Solomon explained that "a fool's voice is known by multitude of words" (Ecclesiastes 5:3). David said, "…I will take heed to my ways, that I sin not with my tongue: I will keep my mouth with a bridle, while the wicked is before me" (Psalms 39:1). On this issue of the tongue, many men are guilty of talking either too much or too quickly. Making rash statements and quick remarks can greatly injure a man's effectiveness as a leader. The Bible says, "A fool uttereth all his mind: but a wise man keepeth it in till afterwards" (Proverbs 29:11).

When I was about eight years old, my mother had to have an operation. Her parents came up to see her and to stay with us kids during that time. I will never forget the words of wisdom that my dear old grandpa gave to me one day while sitting in the swing. He looked at me and said, "Son, remember this. You are the master of your words until they are spoken. Then they become the master of you." As a little boy, it made a huge impression on me. Unfortunately, I did not really begin to understand the impact of that statement until many years later. Rude statements, harsh criticisms, sarcastic replies and insulting comments have no place in the life of a godly man. "There is that speaketh like the piercings of a sword: but the tongue of the wise is health" (Proverbs 12:18).

Make no mistake - there is a thin line between having character and being a coward. My father always reminded me that "Silence is golden, but sometimes it's just plain yellow!" I learned at an early age the impact of the tongue. Sometimes it is necessary to just be quiet. However, there are many men that prefer to remain quiet when the proper course of action would be a bold declaration of truth. They lack the intestinal fortitude to speak out and let their voice be heard. The sign of a godly man is a man that knows when to speak and when not to.

Learning to control one's mind and tongue are two very difficult tasks. These tasks will never be mastered, but we can learn to grow in our walk with the Lord by allowing him to help us in these areas. Another major area of our life where our abilities to control are put to the ultimate test are in our homes. We have all met children that are absolutely out of control. Whose fault is that? The lack of controlled children is a direct reflection of the incompetence of the parents. I never cease to be amazed at the fact that man can train killer whales, lions, tigers, panthers, bears and every other animal in the world. We have all seen the unbelievable reaction to these animals to the slight, almost imperceptible hand gestures and cues coming from the trainer. These animals respond with precise obedience and complete predictability. What is more amazing that though man can train and control these huge animals, they are complete failures many times when it comes to training their children! How can you explain a two hundred pound man giving in to a whining four year old? Who do you suppose is to blame in this situation?

A godly man will produce godly children. The Bible is very clear about that. "Train up a child in the way he should go: and when he is old, he will not depart from it" (Proverbs 22:6). At the ripe old age of one hundred and ten, Joshua on his deathbed assumed full responsibility for the direction his family would take. He told the entire nation of Israel to make their choice. He then reminded himself, his family and his country that as for him and his house, they would serve the Lord. Joshua's leadership in the home was not the product of his leadership in the nation – but visa versa. Joshua's ability to lead his family prepared him to lead an entire nation in the right direction. "As arrows are in the hand of a mighty man; so are children of the youth. Happy is the man that hath his quiver full of them: they shall not be ashamed, but they shall speak with the enemies in the gate" (Psalms 127:4, 5).

Children are impressionable yet intelligent. Just like the arrow, they will fly in the direction they are pointed. Selfish parents yield selfish children. Carnal men produce carnal children. God's plan for the home is for the man to set the tone and lead the family. If Satan can cause the men in the house to fall, the women and children will be very easy victims. "Or else how can one enter into a strong man's house, and spoil his goods, except he first bind the strong man? and then he will spoil his house" (Matthew 12:29). "No man can enter into a strong man's house, and spoil his goods, except he will first bind the strong man; and then he will spoil his house" (Mark 3:27). The problem today is that our strong men are weak, and they are producing a generation of even weaker men. What the father does in moderation, the son will do in excess. As a father of four, two of them being sons, every day is a renewed endeavor to raise them for the Lord to be both real men as well as godly.

Chapter Eight

The Exceptional Man's Giving

"I have shewed you all things, how that so labouring ye ought to support the weak, and to remember the words of the Lord Jesus, how he said, It is more blessed to give than to receive."
(Acts 20:35)

Generosity is a wonderful character trait. In an age of unabashed selfishness, a man's attitude toward giving can be very enlightening. Generosity is a trademark of a godly man. A man that does not readily give what he has is greedy, materialistic and unhappy. In a society that is plagued with a "dog-eat-dog" mentality, men with a giving heart are a refreshing inspiration. A person that is not so obsessed with who they are and what they have, that they are willing to invest in someone else, is a most unusual find. A true test of a man's level of commitment is directly proportionate to his level of giving. "God loveth a cheerful giver" (II Corinthians 9:7).

Selfishness comes in many disguises. When the wife asks you to help her in the kitchen, and you refuse, that is selfishness. When your children ask you repeatedly to help them fix their bicycle, and you keep putting them off, that is a form of selfishness. When the pastor asks you to teach a class or help paint the Sunday School rooms and you make an excuse, that is selfishness. When you see a need and you shut up your bowels of compassion, that is selfishness.

God is not so much interested in how much a man gives as He is in what he has left over. I am afraid that many times, people are so preoccupied at the amount they are giving that they lose scope of what they are keeping. Jesus was more impressed with the widow's two mites than He was with the huge donations by the rich boys. As a child of God, the Scriptures remind us that when God saved us, He bought us. "For ye are bought with a price: therefore glorify God in your body, and in your spirit, which are God's" (I Corinthians 6:20). A man can have two basic attitudes toward giving. One outlook is that of a man that is being billed by God for something he owes. The other attitude is that of a man that is in love with God and wants to show it every chance he gets. When talking to some men, I get the impression that what they have is theirs; and if they want to give God something, that is their prerogative. That is not scriptural at all!

Selflessness

An excellent example of a giving man is the Apostle Paul. Of all the positive character traits that Paul had, one of the most distinguishing attributes was generosity. Paul was not a wealthy man. That is very clear from his many letters. In a letter to the Philippians, he admitted that he knew what it was like to go without. "I know both how to be abased, and I know how to abound: every where and in all things I am instructed both to be full and to be hungry, both to abound and to suffer need" (Philippians 4:12). He had experienced all sides of the financial spectrum. According to Acts 18:2 and 3, Paul was by trade a tentmaker. He had to supplement the gifts of others by making tents when the need arose. The generosity of Paul is seen in his second letter to the Corinthians. He explained to them that he had no desire to be a burden to them. He used the example of a father in chapter 12 verse 14. He compared himself to a father that worked in order for his children to have an inheritance. In verse 15, he makes a powerful statement; a statement that has challenged me on many occasions. Paul said, "And I will very gladly spend and be spent for you. . . ." What an attitude! What generosity! Paul's confession was very short, but it involved more than we will ever know. Paul in essence was telling them that he would very gladly not only give of his belongings, his finances or his assets, but he would also give of himself.

Unlike many men today, they think that if they drop a few bucks in the plate at church once in a while, they have fulfilled their obligations. They have every excuse in the book why they can't tithe on their income. There are so many people today that will spend more time and effort trying to justify their selfishness than just obeying God's word. Churches are closing down. Ministries are suffering. Pastors are living on poverty-level income. Missionaries are struggling to fulfil the Great Commission. And while the world goes to hell, the people of God sit on their wallets with their arms crossed and emphatically declare, "I just can't afford to give anymore!"

Many men spend more on hobbies and recreation than they do on the work of God. They won't think anything of buying a new rifle or shotgun. Bass boats, campers, golf clubs and sporting paraphernalia prices are sky high. Club memberships, 4x4's, vacations and timeshares are not cheap, yet Christian men very readily whip out their pocketbooks to purchase these items. However, let a preacher announce a need from the pulpit, let a missionary stop by that needs financial assistance, or let the church decide to start a building project, and these big spenders suddenly become sober, sour tightwads.

They act offended that they have been asked to give more than they are already giving. They whine and moan about their bills being so high and their salary being so low and give every excuse in the book why they can't contribute to the cause. Amazing isn't it?

The house of Stephanas was an extraordinary household. If we had more families like them, there is no limit to what could be done for God. Paul addressed them in I Corinthians 16:15 by mentioning their uncommon love for the things of God. He greeted them by saying, "I beseech you, brethren, (ye know the house of Stephanas, that it is the firstfruits of Achaia, and that they have addicted themselves to the ministry of the saints,)" What a testimony! What a reputation! They were "ministry addicts!" I especially like that phrase where Paul said, "They have addicted themselves." In other words, Paul didn't addict them. Others in the church didn't draft them or appoint them. They were not voted in by a committee. They addicted themselves! It was something they wanted to do. Ministering for the glory of God was something that they found fulfillment and joy in doing. It was not done out of duty or obligation. It was a pleasure.

Allow me to ask a couple of very pointed questions. If you are a born again child of God, these questions are more than fair. How much time did you give to the ministry of God in the past week? How much time did you spend involved in the furtherance of the gospel? Let me put it this way. How much trouble did you go to in the past week to see the work of God go on? What about this one: If everybody in the church did as much as you did, would the church be here this time next year? Here's another question: If somebody accepts Jesus Christ in your city this week, will you get any credit for it at the Judgment Seat?

Should I Tithe?

The bottom line is this: the success of God's work requires money and time. Lots of it. If the people of God do not finance the work, and if they do not roll up their sleeves and get busy, then who will? If the work of God is not a priority to you, then you need to confront the fact that you have misplaced priorities. Only what is done for Christ will last. If you are spending all of your efforts to accumulate nice things and all of your time is spent having fun, you have missed the most important element of Christianity. When ballplayers make millions of dollars a year to play games, yet missionaries and churches suffer from financial strain, something is terribly wrong. If we could calculate the total amount of funding that the professional sports crowd receives from professing Christians, and compare it to what is given to the ministry, we would be shocked. I will even go so far as to say that if the born again Christians would put their recreation money into the church, we would see a revival break out in our local churches. People would see that we were serious about something of eternal value and would want to learn more about it.

Strangely enough, I'm not only referring to tithing. Though I believe tithing to be both scriptural as well as applicable today, a man's giving should far surpass his tithe. Many people try to dodge the tithing issue by claiming that it was given under the law and is thereby null and void. The only problem with that excuse is that it is not scriptural. Abraham tithed a tenth of all his possessions at least four hundred years before the law was given! It is not a law issue – it is a love issue! For God so loved the world, that he gave… A man's love will result in a man's giving. Solomon said it like this: "Honour the LORD with thy substance, and with the firstfruits of all thine increase:" (Proverbs 3:9). The firstfruits mean the gross, not the net. If you only tithe on what is left, your giving will not amount to very much. Though tithing is Biblical, tithing is just the beginning. I haven't tithed in years. Our family gives much more than a tenth. As my love for God grows, my giving grows. He said in Malachi 3 that there needs to be meat in His house. As long as He has a house, there needs to be meat in it! If the people of God do not keep meat in His house, who will?

When I preach from Malachi chapter three on the principle of tithes and offerings, I am amazed at the people that refuse to believe God on the matter. I have heard every possible interpretation of those verses. The Old Testament principle of sowing and reaping is repeated several times in the New Testament. Malachi 3:10 says, "Bring ye all the tithes into the storehouse, that there may be meat in mine house, and prove me now herewith, saith the LORD of hosts, if I will not open you the windows of heaven, and pour you out a blessing, that there shall not be room enough to receive it." Later on Jesus reiterated this promise with these words, "Give, and it shall be given unto you; good measure, pressed down, and shaken together, and running over, shall men give into your bosom. For with the same measure that ye mete withal it shall be measured to you again" (Luke 6:38).

The way I have always looked at this matter of tithing is actually quite simple. If I am not expected to tithe, but I do it anyway, the only thing I am guilty of is giving money to the work of God that I did not have to. If I am supposed to tithe, and I don't, then I'm guilty of robbing God. As far as I am concerned, that is not even a choice. The principle of sowing and reaping justifies any preaching I may do on the matter of giving. "But this I say, He which soweth sparingly shall reap also sparingly; and he which soweth bountifully shall reap also bountifully" (2 Corinthians 9:6). You will reap what you sow. If you sow to the work of God, you will reap the blessings of God. If you sow materialistic, selfish seed, you will reap a harvest of carnal fruit. It is just that simple.

A Cheerful Giver

The attitude of most people toward giving is so unBiblical. They act as if God is dead and if they give away what they have, they will never get anything else. Their faith in God's daily provision is so weak that they have never even come close to the Biblical concept of a "cheerful giver." To them, giving is not cheerful. It is not a joy. It is not a blessing. Giving is drudgery, a chore, and an obligation. They feel guilty for not giving enough or either they feel depressed for what they did give. They think of ways to get out of giving. Some even go to the lengths that Annanias and Sapphira did in Acts chapter five. They sold some land and then lied to the church about the price. They publicly declared that they were giving it all to the Lord, but kept some back for their own use. They conspired to lie to the preacher and to the church about the transaction and the amount that they sold it for. If you read the story, you will see that God killed them both for their lying, their deceit and their greed. Peter told them that they had not lied to him, but to the Holy Ghost. In their efforts to look spiritual, they both ended up dead.

Their greatest sin was not in keeping back part of the profit from their land sale. Their sin was trying to make it look like they were giving more than they really were. To rob God is one thing. To rob Him and then try to look spiritual while you're doing it is too much! "Be not deceived; God is not mocked: for whatsoever a man soweth, that shall he also reap" (Galatians 6:7). God give us more men that will be willing like Paul to "spend and be spent" for the cause of Christ!

Chapter Nine

The Exceptional Man's Going

"And he said unto them, Go ye into all the world, and preach the gospel to every creature." (Mark 16:15)

Interestingly enough, the first two letters of "godly" is GO. The first two letters of "gospel" is GO. The first two letters of "good" are GO. God's word is filled with admonitions to GO. One of the differences in a common man and *The Exceptional Man* is one is content to stay and the other has a desire to GO. The act of going indicates a destination, a determination, a desire, and deliberation. Going men are men of action. Even a casual reading of the word of God will reveal that there was one common characteristic of all the men God used the most. That trait was they were always going and always pursuing the call of God in their life.

The Great Commission

The greatest command that the Lord Jesus Christ gave to the church involves going. He was standing on the Mount of Olives with His disciples. He was about to ascend back to the

Father. His mind was on one major task – that of the evangelization of the world. After spending the past three and a half years training and preparing His disciples, Jesus left them with one simple command. "And he said unto them, Go ye into all the world, and preach the gospel to every creature" (Mark 16:15). This simple command was left to just a handful of men; men whose lives had been changed by the Lord; men who had experienced His saving power and the transformation that knowing Him can bring. Jesus' final command was for them to take the gospel into the world and share it with every man, woman, boy, and girl.

That command has been one of the most disobeyed commands of the Lord. For some reason, men cannot seem to get into their heads the importance of following this order. To minimize the importance of the godly man's going is to minimize the purpose of the godly man. God's will for godly men involves a purpose and a pursuit of His divine plan. A man that will not go is a man that is not right with God. Many times in the Bible, God vocalized His desire for men that will go. In Isaiah chapter six, God asked the prophet a simple yet many times ignored question. "Also I heard the voice of the Lord, saying, Whom shall I send, and who will go for us? Then said I, Here am I; send me" (Isaiah 6:8). God is still asking that question. Who can He send? Who will go?

It has been said many times, but it is appropriate to say it once more. One of the greatest mistakes King David ever made was the day he stayed at home when he should have been fighting. In II Samuel 11:1 the story begins with this information: "And it came to pass, after the year was expired, at the time when kings go forth to battle, that David sent Joab, and his servants with him, and all Israel; and they destroyed the children of Ammon, and besieged Rabbah. <u>But David tarried still at Jerusalem.</u>" This proved to be one of the worst days of his life. The day David tarried is the day he fell into adultery. Adultery led to an unwanted pregnancy. The pregnancy led to the murder of Uriah. The murder of Uriah led to the death of the newborn baby. One thing led to another, and before it was over, Tamar had been raped. Amnon, the one that raped Tamar, was killed by her brother, Absalom. It was just a matter of time before Absalom was also killed. The whole disaster began the day that kings were supposed to be going forth to battle, and David tarried behind.

It is easy to find volunteers to stay behind, but to find those that are willing to go is becoming a difficult task. The reason for this dilemma is not easy to determine. It might be laziness, but I doubt it. It might be carnality. It could be fear. It is my opinion that the main reason why men do not go is because of apathy. We discussed this in an earlier chapter, but men just don't care. If it does not directly involve them or profit them someway, they are not interested in getting involved. The lack of going men is a direct result of the lack of godly men. A godly man will want to do something to further the work of God. He will not be content just sitting by as a spectator.

Spectators and Participators

The work of God is compiled of two kinds of people: spectators and participators. Just as the spectators at a ballgame can diagnose every mistake and error, those that do nothing in the ministry can quickly tell those that are busy what they are doing wrong. They can advise and instruct, but when it comes down to them actually doing something, you can forget it. It reminds me of the two men that were talking. One was really letting the other man have it. He told him, "You have made a lot of mistakes!" The other man replied, "If you did as much as I did, you'd make mistakes too!" One of the dangers of doing something is there is always the possibility that you will do it wrong. Those that never do anything will never make a mistake. One of my favorite quotes is "I'd rather try and fail than to fail to try."

Going involves risk. Going involves dying to self. Going involves taking your life and your plans and putting them aside for the cause of Christ. God is looking for men that are serious enough about their Christianity to go and tell others of the saving power of Jesus Christ. God wants men who understand that He did not put them here to make them fat and rich. God put us here for a purpose: that purpose is to be an ambassador of Christ. He has given us an extremely sobering task: that task is the ministry of reconciliation. "And all things are of God, who hath reconciled us to himself by Jesus Christ, and hath given to us the ministry of reconciliation;" (II Corinthians 5:18). It is God's desire for every born again Christian to busy themselves with the task of reconciling sinful man with a forgiving God.

God is all powerful and can do anything He wants to do. He could have written the gospel in the constellations. He could have inscribed the gospel on the backs of every leaf. He could have revealed the simple plan of salvation to a lost and dying world a multitude of ways. Instead, He chose to use men to propagate the gospel. His plan for the evangelization of the world relies on godly men GOING. "But ye shall receive power, after that the Holy Ghost is come upon you: and ye shall be witnesses unto me both in Jerusalem, and in all Judaea, and in Samaria, and unto the uttermost part of the earth" (Acts 1:8).

The problem with the whole concept of world missions is a lack of seriousness on the part of God's people. Those that are supposed to give refuse to give, resulting in a shortage of money. Those that are supposed to go refuse to go, resulting in a shortage of missionaries. While the people of God play around and goof off, the world is dying and going to a Christ-less eternity. Whose fault it is that children in foreign lands have never heard the name of Jesus Christ? Whose fault is it that millions are dying every day never having heard a clear presentation of the gospel? Whose fault is it that entire countries are blinded by false religion because they've never had access to the truth? It is the fault of the church! The Lord Jesus Christ commanded the church to further the gospel. He commanded them to tell the whole world that He came and died and rose again for their sins. It is our job as believers to GO!

My Testimony

As a veteran missionary, I am very passionate about this subject of world missions. I suppose I got it honestly, considering that my dad was also in missions. I had the opportunity to grow up in a Christian home. Furthermore, my dad was a pastor and a missionary. In the 1970s, Dad pastored in South Georgia. During the '80s, we were missionaries in the Samoan Islands in the South Pacific and also in the Hawaiian Islands. I grew up with an acute awareness of the spiritual needs of those around me. Life was exciting, and every day was an adventure. We saw things and experienced things that would fill a book. It was early in 1984 when we first arrived in the capital city of Pago Pago, and I was eleven years old. It was a fascinating place with a luscious tropical climate. The island of Tutuila where we lived was only seventeen miles long.

We found a house to rent and settled in to life as missionaries. Just a couple of weeks after arriving there, we were in a laundry mat one day. As my parents did the laundry, my twin sister, my younger brother and I played around outside. While we were there, five young Samoan men walked in for no apparent reason. I felt compelled to witness to them, so I walked over and begin talking with them. After they found out what I had to say, four of them laughed and got up and left. One of them stayed behind to listen. I did the best I could for a while, but finally realized that I needed some reinforcements! I called one of my parents over to help me, and to make a long story short, Villi prayed right there in that laundry mat and asked the Lord to save him. We lost track of Villi for a couple of weeks. One day while we were in town, we bumped into

Villi. He explained that he had been visiting family on another island. He came to our house, and my dad began to disciple him. One thing led to another, and the next thing we knew, Villi showed up at the house with Uiato. Uiato got gloriously saved that night, and the next day he came bringing several of his friends. Before it was over, our living room was filled with Samoans that God had saved and changed.

My days were spent catching crawfish in the mountain streams or building forts in the sugar cane. We would climb up in the mango trees and eat mangos until we were about to burst. We played in the river and learned to peel coconuts with a pickax. In the evenings, I would sit around the table listening to my dad teach the Samoan men how to be godly Christian leaders. As he taught, I would sit and make notes of what he said. Looking back now, I realize what a wealth of knowledge I had access to as a little boy. It was almost like attending Bible College, only more fun! Dad would teach them the Bible, and they would in turn teach us Samoan songs. We would sit around on woven mats and learn new songs and phrases in the Samoan language.

Those days as a young boy were the foundation of a ministry that would develop over a lifetime. I developed a passion for souls that has only increased as the years have passed. From that day in the laundry mat as an eleven year old boy, God lit a fire in my soul that I can't explain. Since that time, I have determined to spend my life showing people how to be saved. It is the greatest life in the world. Watching hurting, broken lives being transformed by the power of the gospel is a sight that never gets old. What is a mystery to me is why men that profess to be born again have to be begged, bribed, pumped and primed to do something for God! Why can't they see the importance of spreading the message of redemption, forgiveness and salvation? What is so complicated about being a vessel in the hand of the Almighty to deliver people from the judgment of God?

After we left Samoa, we went to the island of Oahu in Hawaii. The environment there made an even stronger impression on me. Near our house in Hawaii was a naval base. Every day planes and jets would be flying overhead. I began to develop an interest in flying. My brother and I bought model airplanes and had them hanging from the ceiling in our bedroom. We had Air Force posters on every wall. We learned all the names of the jets and could identify them from miles away. I wrote to the Air Force Academy in Colorado and received a packet of information about what it would take to become a pilot. I made excellent grades, so I began to mentally make plans to go into the Air Force and become a pilot. As the months when on, God began to work in my heart. I felt this tug-of-war taking place within me.

As a young man, I felt this desire to fly a plane. I couldn't get it out of my mind. On the other hand, God began to deal with me about using my life for something more important. After months of wrestling with God, I finally surrendered my life to Him completely when I was about sixteen years old. I knew that night that I would never be an Air Force pilot. I didn't know what I would be doing, but I knew what I wouldn't be doing. Dad had to fly back to Georgia to be with his mother who was very ill. During those six weeks that Dad was gone, I had the frightening but exhilarating privilege to fill the pulpit. I was not a preacher, but Dad felt comfortable leaving me in charge during that time. Those six weeks made a huge impact in my life.

We eventually moved back to Georgia and it was there that I finished high school. Later, I went to Pensacola Christian College for a while in Pensacola, Florida. I studied business and computer science. I really enjoyed it down there, but something was missing in my life. During the summer of 1993, I was sitting in a camp meeting in North Georgia listening to a pastor from Oklahoma. He preached a message entitled "I

Surrender All." I will never forget it as long as I live. As he preached, the Lord began to deal with me about my selfishness. I had surrendered my life to God back in Hawaii as a teenager. Now I was twenty-one years old and something strange was happening to me. I had always told the Lord, "I'll do anything you want me to do – except preach!" I even joked about it. I did not want to be a preacher, or so I thought. My dad was a preacher, his dad was a preacher, and my great-grandfather was a circuit riding preacher in the early 1900s. He traveled around and pastored four quarter-time churches at the same time. I figured that this preacher thing had gone on long enough! I was content to get a high paying job and just be normal. Things were going along fine until God showed up and changed everything.

That hot afternoon in June as that preacher from Oklahoma was preaching, God began to reveal His plan for my life. I found myself at the altar after the message crying out to God to forgive me for being so selfish with my life. He had so graciously saved my soul as a four-year old boy back in 1976. He had allowed me the awesome privilege of being raised in a preacher's home and on the foreign mission field. He had been so good to me and all I could think about was what I wanted to do with my life. I prayed fervently for about two weeks, and on the tenth of July, 1993, I announced my call to preach the gospel. My life suddenly took on a new meaning. I dropped out of Pensacola Christian College and took a position as an Associate Pastor at a church in North Atlanta. Later the Lord moved me back to my home church as the youth leader, and after that I was married. A year later, I decided that I needed to seriously study the word of God to prepare for the ministry. My wife and I moved near Augusta, Georgia, and I began Bible college.

About the same time we moved to Augusta, I left my job and started a construction business with my brother-in-law. At first, it was a bit scary, but God began to bless and in no time at all we were both making over a thousand dollars a week. We were expecting our first child and life was great. During that time, my wife, Grace, and I took a quick vacation down to Savannah. While we were there, we heard about a Missions Conference that was going on nearby. We decided to go and see what was happening. While we were there that week, God began to deal with my heart about becoming a missionary. I was a little surprised actually. Having grown up on the mission field, I somehow felt that I had "done my time." I had a great love for missionaries and mission work, but had never once contemplated being involved in it any more than just in a financial way. During that week, God began to impress upon my heart a burden for the people of South Africa. That was the strange part.

I had never heard of South Africa. I knew nothing about the place. We went home and I told my wife that I felt that God had done something unexplainable in my heart during that week. She was quiet and I let it go. Life continued on and we had another child – a son this time. The construction business was booming and we were making more money than we'd ever seen in our lives. My brother-in-law and I eventually split up and before it was over, we had five crews working full-time. Our third child was born in the fall of 1999. Soon after, my Bible college training ended. For three and a half years I had sat in Bible College and was still as clueless as to what God wanted me to do as I was the day He called me to preach. One thing that didn't make sense was I couldn't get South Africa out of my mind. It just lingered like cheap perfume in an elevator. Something had to give. I couldn't carry on like this.

In January of 2000, I took a survey trip to South Africa. I made God a deal. I told Him that if He would confirm in my heart that He wanted me there, I would go. After ten days of preaching, distributing literature and assisting a couple of missionaries, God confirmed it. I will never be able to explain the peace that flooded my soul when I realized what God had been preparing me for all my life. I went back to Georgia and set my wife down and told her of God's call. I will never forget her reply. She said, "If that is God's will, I'll follow you." We immediately put our house up for sale. I announced at work that I was going to Africa. My men thought I had lost my mind. The business was exploding. My payroll was $8,000 a week, my income had finally hit six digits, and we were just getting started. The sky was the limit and here I was walking away from it all. I sold my F-350 Powerstroke Diesel, crew-cab truck. I sold my wife's Chrysler New Yorker. I sold about half of my tools, and we bought a van. We stepped out by faith and started going around to churches telling them of God's call on our life. We had three small children; two of them were in diapers. God began to open doors, and in less than a year He miraculously raised sufficient monthly support for us to leave for South Africa.

We said our goodbyes and flew to the land of our calling. For five and half years, we served the Lord in the city of Bloemfontein in the Free State Province. God did some amazing things. Many souls were saved. A Bible-believing, soul-winning Baptist church was established. A Bible college was started for the purpose of training men and women for the work of God. The church has a printing ministry and we distributed literally hundreds of thousands of pieces of literature throughout the country. This has been done, not only in South Africa, but also in Nigeria, Ghana, Kenya, Liberia, Lesotho and several other countries throughout the continent of Africa. Our fourth child was born in a hospital in Bloemfontein. The Lord allowed me to write over thirty books and tracts and see several of them translated into the local languages while I was on the field. I had the blessed opportunity to preach in dozens of schools and at the University on several occasions. Lives are being changed and people are finding God's will for their lives still today. The church was turned over to a national pastor and God is still blessing that ministry.

South Africa is considered to be the most dangerous country in the world. It has the highest crime rate in the world with 20,000 murders per year. Violent crime is the norm and poverty abounds. AIDS is killing the people by the millions. Prostitution is legal. Corruption is everywhere. We were robbed on several occasions. People are leaving South Africa by the planeloads and moving to places like Australia, New Zealand, the UK, Canada, and America. Unemployment is 40% and growing. That once beautiful country has been ravished by Satan and by sin until there is hardly anywhere one can go and be safe. The occult is flourishing. Ancestor worship and witchdoctors are revered and respected to the highest degree.

After serving in South Africa, God called me back to pastor Pleasant View Baptist Church in Taylors, South Carolina. Pleasant View is a wonderful church that has a Boy's Academy, a Christian School, and hosts a tremendous Camp Meeting twice a year. If I had it to do all over again, I would still go to South Africa. I was commanded to go. The Great Commission is not a suggestion; it is a command. It is up to godly men to carry the gospel of the Lord Jesus Christ. It is countries like South Africa that Christ had in mind when He gave the Great Commission. "When Jesus heard it, he saith unto them, They that are whole have no need of the physician, but they that are sick: I came not to call the righteous, but sinners to repentance" (Mark 2:17). You may not be called to go to South Africa, but you are called to go somewhere. It might be across the sea or across the street. The world is dying and going to hell without God, and it is our problem. What are you going to do about it?

"And I sought for a man among them, that should make up the hedge,
and stand in the gap before me for the land, that I should not destroy it:
but I found none." (Ezekiel 22:30)

Chapter Ten

The Exceptional Man's Growing

"But grow in grace, and in the knowledge of our Lord and Saviour Jesus Christ."
(2 Peter 3:18)

One of the most disappointing facts of many Christian men's lives is that they never continue to grow in the Lord. They get saved they are excited for a while, and everything is new to them. They get involved in a Bible believing church. They take their Bible and sit on the front row and listen to everything with childlike eagerness. They are many times like a sponge that just soaks up the water of the word. Nothing offends them and they like it straight and strong. "As newborn babes, desire the sincere milk of the word, that ye may grow thereby:" (I Peter 2:2).

Stale and Stagnant Saints

As time goes on, their hunger for the word begins to diminish. They look around at all the more mature, stable believers in the church and realize that they look a little foolish.

They begin to lose their fire and their zeal. After a while, they have settled in to a groove that is more or less up to par with the other church members. They don't mind sitting further back in the church. If they forget to bring their Bible, it is no big deal. Their once receptive heart slowly becomes a heart that is critical and cautious. When the preacher preaches, he's not always right. It's just his interpretation. They no longer feel excited about their salvation. They actually forget what it was like to be unsaved. They lose that glimmer in their eye and that bounce in their step. They rarely stand and testify of God's goodness or an answer to prayer. They don't have as many prayer requests as they used to.

Their relationship with the pastor becomes a little more distant. He's a good man, but sometimes he comes across a little to strong. It's hard for a man that came from a life of sin and scars to relate to the preacher. He knows a lot more about the Bible and his confidence in the Word is intimidating. He's always trying to get people motivated and charged up, but he just doesn't realize what it's like to work a real job. Church becomes routine. If I miss a service or two, it just doesn't matter that much. The apathy continues and the growth comes to a screeching halt. This new convert has now become a seasoned believer that has gone as far with God as he will ever go. Sometimes this process takes six months. Sometimes it takes a few years. Unfortunately, it will invariably happen sooner or later. Our churches are filled with stagnant Christians. What they know about the Bible could be written on a piece of paper and stuffed into a thimble. They have no idea what the Bible says about the major doctrines of the faith, and they couldn't care less. They're saved and on their way to Heaven, and that's all they need to know.

Growing In Knowledge

A godly man will have a desire to be more godly. A Christian man should have a desire to be more Christ-like. One of the most heartbreaking things to see is a carnal man that is happy being carnal. He knows he's got a lot to learn, but he has no desire to be more than what he is right now. His attitude toward growth is one of complete ignorance. Knowledge is power. That explains why we have such weak men. They are lacking knowledge. They are ignorant of the word of God, the will of God, the ways of God and the work of God. They have no desire to understand the truths of God's word. They are not the least bit interested in solving the mysteries contained within the Scripture. It seems that their viewpoint is, "If I don't know it, then I won't have to give an account for it." The Bible teaches that to whom much is given, much is required (Luke 12:48).

To assume that ignorance is safety is a huge mistake. We are commanded to learn and to study. "Study to shew thyself approved unto God, a workman that needeth not to be ashamed, rightly dividing the word of truth" (2 Timothy 2:15). The purpose of studying the Word is to be able to properly discern its truths. When we are able to properly discern its truths, we can then properly apply them to our lives. When we properly apply them to our lives, we become conformed into the image of Christ. That is God's ultimate goal for our lives. He wants us to be just like His Son. "For whom he did foreknow, he also did predestinate to be conformed to the image of his Son. . . ." (Romans 8:29).

It is impossible for a spiritual dwarf to be like Christ! A man that has not grown in his faith is completely at a disadvantage. How can you be like Someone that you don't know anything about? How can you please God if your knowledge of His word is so limited? Paul urged Timothy to study in order to show himself approved unto the Lord. Growing in grace and knowledge is not so you can impress others. The purpose of growth is so you can glorify God.

Another huge benefit of spiritual growth is the ability to discern truth and error. Many false prophets are in the world today. "Beloved, believe not every spirit, but try the spirits whether they are of God: because many false prophets are gone out into the world" (I John 4:1). If you do not know your Bible, you are in great danger of being deceived by lies and perverted gospel. The statistics are astounding of the number of people that get ensnared by the cults. These are people that come from sound, Bible-believing churches. They simply did not know what the Bible said. Someone came along preaching another gospel and they fell for it.

Practical Applications

As a teenager, I would accompany my Dad as he visited people in their homes. I learned to witness to people from every nationality and religious background. I watched my Dad expertly handle the Scriptures, and it gave me a great love for the word of God. It also made a huge impact in my life when I realized that no matter what people believe, the final truth can be discovered in the word of God. It whetted my appetite for a deeper knowledge of the Bible. I was not content to just read it. I wanted to know it and understand it. I wanted to be able to sit down with anybody from any walk of life and find the answers to their problems.

I distinctly remember a time when I was about fifteen years of age and my parents were not at home. A couple of Jehovah's Witnesses knocked at our door and proceeded to try and sell me some literature. I remember the feeling I experienced when I asked them did they believe that Jesus was God in the flesh. Of course they denied it. I then proceeded to show them from their own perverted New World Translation that Jesus was indeed Jehovah. I first took them to Isaiah 43:11 where their Bible read, "I –I am Jehovah, and beside me there is no savior." I asked them did they believe that verse. They assured me that Jehovah was the only Savior. I then took them to Acts 4:10-12 where Peter was preaching about Jesus Christ. In verse 12, Peter said, "Furthermore, there is no salvation in anyone else, for there is not another name under heaven that has been given among men by which we must get saved" *(New World Translation – 1960)*. Needless to say, they were absolutely speechless. From their own book I proved to them that Jesus was indeed Jehovah. I asked them to explain the discrepancy in the Scriptures. They couldn't. They blushed and looked down and eventually left. Later on that evening, they came back to the house for the sole purpose of congratulating my Dad for training his son in the Scriptures. They told him that they had no answer to my questions. I knew they wouldn't. I had seen my Dad do that same thing on several occasions, and I listened intently and memorized in my Bible where those verses were.

Once I realized that my knowledge of the Bible could directly affect the eternal destiny of someone, it changed my whole outlook. I was no longer happy with my little "Awards" Bible. I worked and saved my money and bought myself an Open Bible with all the study guides and concordances. I began to study my Bible and mark passages in it and familiarize myself with it. I made notes in the front of my Bible where I could quickly find verses to dispute the error and false doctrines that surrounded us. People were confused because they had never learned their Bible. If I had a question, I would study my Bible and read commentaries. I read my Bible all the way through for the first time when I was just fifteen years old. I had made a New Year's resolution on the first of January, 1987 to read my Bible all the way through. With the Lord's help and a lot of determination, I accomplished that goal on November 15th, just ten months and fifteen days later. I was so excited that I wrote it down in the front of my Bible.

I still have that Bible, and it is almost too worn out to use anymore. I developed a huge amount of respect for the men of God that I would encounter that had a better than average understanding of Scripture. As a teenager, I envied their wealth of Bible knowledge. I wanted to know everything they knew overnight. God's word became a very central part of my life. Memorization, study and research only served to increase my desire to know God's word. Little did I know what God had in store for me later on in life.

While laboring in South Africa, I had the opportunity to have what is called a "Question and Answer Session." A school would invite me to do a public, impromptu service where the students were allowed to ask me any question at all. I was once asked to do this for five days in a row at one of the local high schools. Imagine the adrenaline rush of facing a thousand high school kids and not knowing what question they are going to throw at you. It was a memorable time. I had the time of my life as one young person after another asked me a question that had been bothering them. All I had with me was my worn out Bible that I had used since I was a teenager myself. I was asked every question imaginable. I was asked about Harry Potter, smoking, homosexuality, dating, hell, judgment, and everything in between. With the Lord's help, I was able to find the answer to every single question in my Bible. I would simply answer their questions with a Bible verse or two and then ask them if that answered their question.

Amazingly enough, they were satisfied with the answers. I didn't give them my opinion or twist the verses to fit the situation. I just read the verses, and God's word did the work. After about the third day, a beautiful young lady approached me after the session. She growled and stomped her foot. I asked her what her problem was. She said to me, "I'm mad at you!" I asked her why. She said, "Every time we ask you a question, you have the answer!" It was then that I realized that they had been trying to trap me. I just smiled and told her that it pays to know your Bible. She did not know that I had been underlining verses and marking those passages in my

Bible for over twenty years. I do not have all the answers, but thank the Lord, He does! What is better is that He has shared them with us in detail in the pages of the Bible. Too bad most men don't know how to find them. Having a Bible won't do you any good if you can't find what you are looking for!

Apollos

There are several examples of godly men in the Bible that continued to grow, even after they had achieved some level of spirituality. One great example that comes to my mind is Apollos. The Bible describes him in Acts 18:24 as "… a certain Jew named Apollos, born at Alexandria, an eloquent man, and mighty in the scriptures, came to Ephesus." Luke goes on to write, "This man was instructed in the way of the Lord; and being fervent in the spirit, he spake and taught diligently the things of the Lord, knowing only the baptism of John." The Bible says that "…he began to speak boldly in the synagogue: whom when Aquila and Priscilla had heard, they took him unto them, and expounded unto him the way of God more perfectly."

Get the picture here. Apollos was an eloquent man. This indicates that he was an intelligent man and capable of speaking the Word fluently and with effectiveness. Quite a compliment, coming from Luke the physician. Luke goes on to describe Apollos as "mighty in the scriptures." This was another huge compliment. I wouldn't mind going down in history as either eloquent or mighty in Scriptures – or both! The next verse explains further that he was instructed in the way of the Lord and a man of fervency. We desperately need more men that fit that description in our day and age. He also spake and taught the things of God with diligence. He was not a slacker, and he was not lazy in his ministry. He was on fire and running full blast. However, there was a problem. He was off on some doctrinal issues. He was teaching some things that were not exactly right.

When Aquila and his wife Priscilla heard Apollos preaching, they were impressed with his personality, his presentation, and his perseverance. They obviously invited him home with them and began to explain the Scriptures more accurately. The impressive thing is – he listened! He actually humbled himself and allowed himself to be taught. Amazing! When was the last time you admitted you didn't have it all together? This man is an excellent example of a godly man that continued to grow in the Lord.

Paul encouraged Timothy to find faithful men and teach them everything he had learned from Paul. "And the things that thou hast heard of me among many witnesses, the same commit thou to faithful men, who shall be able to teach others also" (2 Timothy 2:2). This is a fascinating verse. Cleverly hidden in this verse are the amazing results of four generations of godly men. Watch closely how this works. "And the things that thou (Timothy, second generation) has heard of me (Paul, first generation) among many witnesses, the same commit thou to faithful men, (Timothy's disciples, third generation) who shall be able to teach others also (fourth generation)."

Can you see the awesome responsibility to learn more and to grow in the knowledge of the Lord Jesus? If you do not learn from those around you, how will you teach your sons and those around you to be more godly? Do you realize that if you have a careless, apathetic attitude toward growth that the process of committing to faithful men will die with you? If you don't care about knowing God's word, what chance do your sons have of knowing it? Children imitate their parents; sons emulate their fathers.

Growing in Grace

Grace is such a beautiful word. We sing of God's grace. We thank Him for His grace. We are saved by grace. It is because of the grace of God that we are alive today. So what does it mean to "grow in grace"? It means taking on the more Christ-like attributes. It is amazing how vulgar and crude men can be in their unsaved condition. Some people's idea of a man is quite shocking when compared to the Biblical description. To the world, a man is a creature that smells like a mule and cusses like a sailor. He hollers at his kids, cheats on his wife, kicks his dog and drinks like a fish. He never shows any manners. He doesn't use deodorant or brush his teeth. He walks around with his shirt off and eats with his fingers. He keeps greasy hair and never grooms himself. To some people, a real man is more like a Neanderthal.

Many men, I'm afraid, are so fearful of being labeled a sissy that they shy away from any public profession of Christianity. I once had an old pickup truck with a bumper sticker on the back window. It read, "Real Men Love Jesus!" You can imagine the looks I got when I would drive up on a job site. Being a godly man does not mean you are a wimp. Having manners and treating people with respect is not the trademarks of a wimp. A godly man will understand the balance in masculinity and graciousness. A man can be gracious without putting his manliness in jeopardy. You don't have to run over people and bully your way around to be a man. You don't have to smell like a hog pen and have grease caked under your nails to be a real man. They sell cologne, deodorant and shoe polish in the men's department. Being dirty, bossy, hateful, and illiterate is not being a man.

A godly man will be a man that is both a man and godly. He will cherish his wife. He will love his children. He will offer a woman his chair. He will hold the door for ladies. He will not insult people. He will not offend them with his appearance. He is polite, well mannered, groomed, clean and kind. He will be a gentleman. He will make an honest effort to represent Christ in every aspect of his life. A godly man will not drink alcoholic beverages. A godly man will not use tobacco. Tobacco is unhealthy, unsightly and offensive. It also hinders your testimony as a Christian. A basic rule to remember is where there is smoke, there is fire. And where there is fire, there is destruction! Your body is the temple of the Holy Ghost. Treat it like one!

Forbearance will be a huge part of the godly man's life. He will not lose his temper and scream at people. He will not start fights. There is a huge difference in starting a fight and protecting yourself or your family. The Biblical admonition that says if someone smites you on your right cheek to turn the other also is a very good example. If someone slaps you on your right cheek, they are either using their left hand or they are hitting you with the back of their right hand. Either way, their purpose was not to hurt you but to insult you. Jesus told his disciples to ignore personal insults. Pay no attention to people who have no class or no decency. Ignore them and as much as lieth within you, live peaceably with all men. (Romans 12:18).

On the other hand, protecting yourself against dangerous men is not condemned in the Scriptures. I own a firearm for the very same reason that a cow has horns. Cows are grass-eating animals but they have horns to insure that they can eat grass in peace. I would not hesitate to inflict bodily harm if my life or the life of my family was at stake. God's word tells me that a man that will not provide for his family is worse than an infidel, and that includes providing them with security, protection, and safety. However, neither a fighting man nor a brawling man is a godly man. A godly man will keep his mouth shut and his hands to himself. A godly man will also defend himself. An exceptional man knows when to act and when not to.

Gracious men are in huge demand. We need men with level heads and clear minds. Men with gentle spirits and humble attitudes are scarce. As a godly man, it should be your desire to grow in grace and in knowledge of the Lord Jesus Christ. Walk like He would walk. Talk like He would talk. Treat people the way He would. In doing so, you will please the Lord and influence other people. The more you focus on your own personal growth, the more God will reveal to you about yourself. He will help you overcome bad habits and ungodly character traits. As time goes on, you will find yourself becoming more and more like Christ. An exceptional man is a gentleman. He is a gracious man and he is a growing man. That is what makes him so exceptional.

Chapter Eleven

The Exceptional Man's Guarding

"When a strong man armed keepeth his palace, his goods are in peace:"
(Luke 11:21)

    Carelessness is a dangerous thing. A man that takes for granted his walk with the Lord is in serious danger of stumbling. It goes without saying, but I'll say it anyway. Satan has his sights on every God-fearing man, woman, boy, and girl. If he can cause a child of God to lose sight of the magnitude of the battle we are embroiled in, he has accomplished a great victory. Satan does not appreciate godly men. His attitude toward them today is the same as it was with Job. He is just waiting for the opportunity to devour each and every Christian. His tactics are effective and his success is astounding. We constantly hear news of men of God that have fallen prey to his devices. It is a sobering thought to realize that nobody is exempt from his temptations.

You are a Target

Satan does not fight fair. He bides his time until we are at our weakest point, and then he strikes. A perfect example of his cowardly strategy is demonstrated in Matthew chapter four. Jesus has been praying and fasting in the wilderness. For forty days He has spent time alone with God. He has had no interaction with other men. He has had nothing to eat. He is tired and hungry. Guess who shows up? The devil came to Him and three times tried to tempt Him to sin. He first attacked the Lord in the area where He would be the most vulnerable – the lust of the flesh. He knew that Jesus was hungry, so that is where he started first.

His next two temptations covered the other two realms of man's weakness: the lust of the eyes and the pride of life. Every sin that you will ever commit will fit under one of these three categories. Younger men battle the lust of the flesh. Middle aged men deal more with the lust of the eyes and materialism. Older men have to contend with a constant battle against the pride of life and their accomplishments and legacy. Satan used all three areas to tempt the Lord. Each time, Jesus was on guard and was able to repel the influences of the devil. It is sobering to realize that even God in the flesh was not exempt from Satanic temptation. You can guarantee that you will not escape him either.

Knowing your weakest areas should prompt you to be much more careful in guarding those areas. You can believe that Satan knows when you are the weakest and where you are the weakest. He doesn't waste his time tempting you in areas where you are strong. He goes for the jugular and a sure kill. He doesn't get in a hurry, but when he strikes, it can be deadly if you are not on guard. The writer of Hebrews realized that we all have weights in our lives and sins which doth so easily beset us (Hebrews 12:1). We all have areas in our life where we are more vulnerable than others. It would behoove us to know our weaknesses and guard against the devil's temptations in those areas.

An excellent verse that commands us to watch our step is Ephesians 5:15. "See then that ye walk circumspectly, not as fools, but as wise." That word "circumspectly" means diligently, accurately, exactly. In order to better understand the concept of walking circumspectly, imagine a ten foot high brick wall. On either side of that wall is a vicious pit bull. On top of the wall is a cat, walking from one end to the other. Just as that cat would walk "circumspectly," we are commanded to walk the same way in the world. A wise man will watch where he is going, every step of the way, realizing that one wrong step can bring sudden destruction.

The Word of God tells us that the heart is deceitful above all things and desperately wicked. (Jeremiah 17:9). To think that you are above being deceived is a huge mistake. Many a man has fallen prey to the prideful assumption that they are above being tricked by the devil. In fact, every time we sin we have been tricked. We have been tricked into believing that we can get by with it. We have believed his lie that nobody will find out. We have been tricked into thinking that we can sin and it will not affect us in any way. What a liar Satan is! Everything he says is a lie. Jesus called him the father of lies (John 8:44).

Establishing Safeguards

One of the biggest mistakes men make is the failure to establish some boundaries in their personal lives. To live without safeguards and protective perimeters is to live recklessly and foolishly. Many men enjoy their freedom just a little bit too much. They have the attitude that because they are adults, they have no restrictions and can do what they want. Though they may be adults, and though they may have the freedom to make their own decisions, there needs to be some accountability somewhere. A man that realizes his weaknesses and makes no precautions to keep himself protected is a fool. Paul urged God's people to exercise care in this area of their life. "But put ye on the Lord Jesus Christ, and make not provision for the flesh, to fulfil the lusts thereof" (Romans 13:14).

As a Christian man, there are some things that I simply will not do in order to protect myself from the devil's fiery darts. It is not because I do not trust myself; it is because I do not trust the devil. It has been his desire since my birth to destroy me. He will stop at nothing to cause me to fall. He will resort to any tactic he can use to bring about my destruction. If I am not careful, he will be successful. I refuse to be alone with another woman. I will not counsel a woman without my wife present. I will not ride in a car with a woman other than my wife. Not only does this protect my testimony, but it also protects me from temptations. I have been warned in Ephesians 4:27, "Neither give place to the devil." That means that I should not give him an opportunity to tempt me. It has always been my most successful strategy at fighting temptations. Instead of stressing myself over resisting the temptation, I simply remove the temptation. Instead of trying to figure out how to overcome ungodly lusts, I just remove the object of the lust.

Dating Guidelines

While my wife and I were dating, we had an unusual agreement. We agreed to wait until our wedding day to have our first kiss. For us it was a safeguard. I realize that in this day and age, dating and kissing is synonymous. We agreed to keep our relationship as pure as possible and free of physical contact and sexual gratification. We managed to court for eighteen months without kissing or necking. Difficult? Not really. You see, we had also agreed to another method of accomplishing our goal of purity. We didn't single date. We did not get in a car and go out for the evening alone. If we went out, we went on a double date – with either her parents or mine. Her parents and my parents were very strict. It is an understatement to acknowledge that with our parents around, the temptation to get physical was kept to a minimum! Crazy? Maybe. But I can tell you one thing - it worked! When we got married, we kissed for the first time at the wedding altar. By the grace of God, we were both virgins. We just recently celebrated eleven years of marriage, and it has been one continuous honeymoon. Even after having four children, my toes still curl up when I kiss my wife! Why? Because we set up some boundaries when we were dating, and it paid off.

Some people mock and laugh when I relate to them our dating experience. What they don't know is that they are the ones that are wrong. I have the Bible to back up my safeguards. They don't. Notice what God said about sexual guidelines. "Now concerning the things whereof ye wrote unto me: It is good for a man not to touch a woman" (I Corinthians 7:1). I looked that verse up in the Greek, and sure enough, it means exactly what it says. Here is another verse: "For by means of a whorish woman a man is brought to a piece of bread: and the adulteress will hunt for the precious life. Can a man take fire in his bosom, and his clothes not be burned? Can one go upon hot coals, and his feet not be burned? So he that goeth in to his neighbour's wife; whosoever toucheth her shall not be innocent" (Proverbs 6:26-29). Here is a question you might want to answer: If touching a married woman is a form of adultery, wouldn't touching an unmarried woman be a form of fornication? You can do what you want to. I'd rather be safe than sorry.

Pornography

Another Satanic attack that Christian men have to fight is this medium of pornography. Pornography is a $57 billion a year industry. Millions of people are secretly involved in the sin of pornography. It is estimated that there are over 372 million pornographic web pages on the internet. Note these unbelievable statistics. These statistics have been derived from a number of different reputable sources including Google, WordTracker, PBS, MSNBC, NRC, and Alexa research.

- Porn revenue is larger than all combined revenues of all professional football, baseball and basketball franchises.
- US porn revenue exceeds the combined revenues of ABC, CBS, and NBC ($6.2 billion)
- Child pornography generates $3 billion annually
- Men admitting to accessing pornography at work - 20%
- US adults who regularly visit Internet pornography websites - 40 million
- Promise Keeper men who viewed pornography in last week - 53%
- Christians who said pornography is a major problem in the home - 47%
- Adults admitting to Internet sexual addiction - 10%
- Average age of first Internet exposure to pornography - 11 years old
- Largest consumer of Internet pornography - 12-17 age group
- 15-17 year olds having multiple hard-core exposures - 80%
- 8-16 year olds having viewed porn online - 90% (most while doing homework)

We are talking about the exceptional man's guarding. A wise man will realize that setting up safeguards in his sexual life will result in sexual purity. A man that does not watch his step when he is in a potentially compromising situation is playing with fire. There are literally dozens of good filters that a person can install on their computer that will protect them from the wiles of the devil. What are a few bucks each month to spend on a safeguard that can potentially save your testimony, marriage, and effectiveness for God? A man that is into pornography cannot have the power of God on his life! The internet is a powerful tool and can be used in many great ways. It is also a trap that Satan is using to kill off an entire generation of godly men. Beware!

Television

Another very effective tool of the devil is the television. The programs that are shown on the TV are the epitome of worldliness. The hidden agendas behind the shows are so unscriptural that they are not really even hidden anymore. Fornication, adultery, nudity, swearing, drunkenness, homosexuality and violence saturate almost every movie and program. There are very few Christian men that would allow the scenes and language that are depicted on the television to transpire within their homes. For some reason, because it is on a screen, it is OK. Profanity and sexual innuendoes are so common that even the youngest child could not escape the subconscious programming of Hollywood. Christianity is mocked; God is denied; sin is glorified, and wicked men are the heroes.

Thankfully, my dad threw the television out of our home back in 1976. He literally threw it out. I remember helping him take it to the landfill. Just six weeks later, God called my dad to preach. A few months later, I was saved. I grew up without the demonic influence of the "hell-ivision." While my wife and I were dating, we both agreed to never allow a television in our home. We have kept that promise, and God has blessed us in so many ways. Our children are learning to draw. They read books, build forts and play for hours as content as anything. Sometimes we just gather around the piano as a family and learn songs to sing in church. Just as I refuse to let unbelievers and government officials educate my children, I refuse to let Hollywood brainwash them. To sit my children down in front of that boob-tube would be the height of irresponsibility and carnality.

Guarding Your Home

It is amazing how stupid men can be when it comes to guarding their home. They know good and well what they were involved in as a kid. They remember all the lies and deceit and the things they did to fool their parents. But for some reason, they think their children are perfect little angels that would never do anything like that. You need to wake up man! "Foolishness is bound in the heart of a child. . . ." (Proverbs 22:15). Children today are losing their innocence a long time before you lost yours! According to the statistics above, 90% of kids between the age of 8 and 16 have viewed pornography online. Young people today are learning the "facts of life" from their playmates at unbelievably young ages. There are several huge influences on your children. One is their friends. Your children's innocence can be completely abolished in a few hours with the wrong children. My wife and I are extremely careful of who we allow our children to play with. The kids across the street can introduce your child to a sin that they will battle for the rest of their lives. From experience I can assure you that sometimes the worst kids your children can be around are the church kids. Just because their parents are pastors or deacons doesn't mean anything! Keep your guard up and your eyes peeled. Satan wants your kids! "No man can enter into a strong man's house, and spoil his goods, except he will first bind the strong man; and then he will spoil his house" (Mark 3:27).

It is my belief that the parents that are careful in their own life will be careful when it comes to their children. A man that is careless in his choice of friends will not care who his children choose for friends. Friends can destroy you, and they can destroy your children. The Bible story of Amnon who raped his half-sister, Tamar, did so under the guidance of his friend. "But Amnon had a friend, whose name was Jonadab, the son of Shimeah David's brother: and Jonadab was a very subtil man" (II Samuel 13:3). You had better know who your children's friends are!

The Danger of Daycare

One of the most destructive elements that Satan ever conceived is the world's version of the daycare concept. Why a man and a woman would want to have a child, and then turn it over to a complete stranger to raise is beyond my comprehension. They not only teach your children how to go to the potty and how to color pretty pictures, but they are teaching them a whole lot of other things. Many of our daycares employ pedophiles and sexual perverts. God's command to "train up a child in the way he should go. . . ." (Proverbs 22:7), does not mean to sub-contract your parenting to someone else. God never intended for the home to be split up all day the way homes are now. The mother has her job, the dad has his, and the kids are thrown to the lions in the process. God warned that in the last days, people would have "unnatural affection." That is so descriptive of a mother that takes her newborn baby and leaves it at a kennel for the whole day, and then goes off to pursue her career. How messed up can you get? If that is not misplaced priorities, what is?

I would rather live in a travel trailer on the backside of a pecan orchard and drive a horse and buggy, than to have a nice house, nice car, and a two salary income while my kids are raised in a daycare. Never in a million years! Our men are allowing this because they like the extra money and the nice things. Parents today are offering up their children on the altar of materialism. They are throwing their kids away so they can fulfill their wants and have a more comfortable lifestyle. An exceptional man is a man that will be the breadwinner for his family so his wife can stay at home where she belongs and raise his kids for God. A man with a wife that doesn't want to stay at home has more than one set of problems on his hand. Notice the trademarks of a whorish woman according to Solomon. In Proverbs 7:11, he described her as "...loud and stubborn; her feet abide not in her house:" Paul commanded Titus to teach the women "to be discreet, chaste, keepers at home, good, obedient to their own husbands, that the word of God be not blasphemed" (Titus 2:5). I wonder how many women are blaspheming the word of God by violating this command!

The Public School Fiasco

What about your child's education? Who do you suppose is responsible to teach your child how to read and write? Do you think that is your responsibility or the governments? When God allowed you and your wife to conceive and give birth to a child, do you suppose it was His will for the unbelieving teachers in your town to educate them? *The Exceptional Man* will give more than two minutes consideration to the quality of education that his children will receive. The schools are filled with teachers and educators that promote every ungodly agenda under the sun. Humanism, evolution, socialism, sex education, political correctness, and that is just the beginning.

The schools will not permit prayer or Bible reading. They will not promote patriotism. They are re-writing the textbooks and American history. They pass out condoms in the halls and promote immorality. What blows my mind is that Bible believing, born-again Christians send their children there to be brainwashed by that crowd! Do they not realize that their children are the next generation of Christianity? Can they not see that all Satan has to do to eliminate Christianity is to infiltrate the innocent, impressionable minds of our youth?

What is the solution, you may ask. Well, I hate to make it sound so simple, but it is quite profound actually. The solution to the public school fiasco is either a church-based Christian school or home-school. Believe it or not, that is the way God-fearing Christians educated their children up until a few hundred years ago. Notice whose responsibility it is to educate the children. "And thou shalt love the LORD thy God with all thine heart, and with all thy soul, and with all thy might. And these words, which I command thee this day, shall be in thine heart: And *thou shalt teach them diligently unto thy children*, and shalt talk of them when thou sittest in thine house, and when thou walkest by the way, and when thou liest down, and when thou risest up" (Deuteronomy 6:5–7). According to these verses, the teaching process is an all day thing. How can a parent teach their children the commandments of God all day long if they are in the world's clutches all day long? How can a woman obey God's command in Titus 2 to "love her children" if she ships them off to the heathen for their education?

Our society has become so unscriptural that even the church has accepted their way of thinking. There is not one single shred of evidence in the Scriptures of a public school concept. The public schools are a result of a cleverly laid scheme to capture the hearts and minds of Christian youth. It began many years ago in a one room schoolhouse with the Parson as the teacher. As time went on, parents relinquished more and more power to the local government. They lost control of the curriculum, the methods of education and eventually their own children. Now, a school can assist a student in performing an abortion without notifying the parents. They can pass out contraceptives without the parent's permission. The school has more parental authority than the parents do. They can call in the authorities and have parents arrested for disciplining their children. The public school system is a shame and a disgrace. It is an affront to God and everything that God stands for. Yet, so called Christians will send their children to these schools; blindly submitting to Satan's scheme for complete control of their young people.

    For those that doubt the effectiveness of a Christian school or a home-school as a viable alternative, have no fear. The effectiveness of the public school to churn out humanist, evolutionist, liberals, atheists, perverts, and illiterate slobs has been dully established. If that is your preference, so be it. I had the privilege of being educated at home for seven years. The other years were spent in church-operated Christian schools. I have never felt disadvantaged or inferior because my parents chose Christian education for me. In fact, I feel that due to the protective environment of the home, my time was better spent. Instead of learning how to play hooky, I learned how to play the piano, the guitar, the banjo and several other instruments. While other kids were busy painting the town red, I was learning watercolors and oil painting and got pretty good at it. When some teenagers were writing their names on the overpasses and water towers with spray paint, I was writing gospel songs to sing at church. As the boys were out laying tracks in the street with their hot-rod, I was in the recording studio with my family laying down tracks of Christ-honoring music. As I said, I don't feel the least bit inferior. Thankful? Yes. Loved? Definitely. Inferior? Never!

    At the church where I pastor, we have a small, Christian Academy on the church property. Many of our families still home school their children, even with a good, Bible-based Christian Academy available. Shielding our youth from the wickedness of the public school system is a high priority. You see, as a father, it is my responsibility to guard my children from the warped viewpoints of the world. It's high time men wake up and get their heads out of the sand. Your children are a heritage from the Lord (Psalms 127:3). Men had better take their job as stewards seriously. To find a man that is serous about his children and his wife and the influences in his home is rare. A guarding man is indeed an exceptional man.

Conclusion

Much could be said about the exceptional man. This book is by no means an exhaustive look at the topic. I am sure that most of the things addressed in this book have already been said by many other preachers and authors. It is simply my heart's desire to see a generation of men raised up in these last days that will stand and be counted for God. That will first require a genuine salvation experience. This is addressed in detail in the epilogue. It will also require a sincere realization that God needs men to further His work. When a man is saved and faces the fact that God has a plan for his life, his life suddenly takes on a whole new meaning. He now has a purpose for living. He now has the Holy Spirit dwelling within him to help him become a godly man.

Once you discover God's plan for you life and begin to walk with Him, God will reveal to you everything you need to know. He has promised to lead you and guide you and to walk with you to help you accomplish His will. Life may be difficult at times. People may not understand the path you've chosen. God's word is a detailed roadmap for you to live by. Being an exceptional man is possible. Being used of God to help others is possible. By following God, listening to His Spirit, and living a daily life according to His word, you can become an exceptional man: A man that is bold, balanced and Biblical.

Epilogue

The Exceptional Man's Gospel

"And for me, that utterance may be given unto me, that I may open my mouth boldly, to make known the mystery of the gospel," (Ephesians 6:19)

No doubt the topics addressed in this book have created a kaleidoscope of responses. As I began to write, God revealed to me the many areas in my own life that do not measure up to His standard. God has shown me so many things that I need to fix in myself and areas that need repair and improvement. This book is the result of a burning passion to see myself, as well as all men, used of God. In recent days, my heart has been broken at the state of men in general. I cannot decide which is more pitiful: the fact that there are so few men that are living for God, or the fact that they don't even seem to notice. What is sad is that most Christian men feel that they are right where they are supposed to be, doing just what they are supposed to be doing. Their wives are crying themselves to sleep at night over their condition. Their kids are going to the dogs. Their pastor is pulling his hair out trying to figure out how to change things.

And the whole time, the men are carrying on in "la-la land" with no clue whatsoever at how short of the mark they have fallen.

I will acknowledge that part of the problem is ignorance. They've never been taught what a godly man is supposed to be. Another problem is a lack of role models. The best way to show how crooked a stick is would be to put a straight one down beside it. If all the men in the church are crooked, there is no way men can know they are spiritual dwarfs. Other causes for the dismal state of manhood today are a mixture of pride, selfishness, arrogance, laziness and apathy. Those attitudes have already been addressed. If our men can rid themselves of these ungodly character traits, we might just see a revival break out in our homes and churches.

Man's Number One Problem

Having said all that, I feel that the largest cause of the state of men today is actually quite simple. Though simple, it is definitely not to be overlooked. To overlook this part of the equation would be a disaster. As a fourth generation Baptist preacher, a second generation missionary, a student of the word of God and a man that has been walking with God for thirty years, I have a verdict to pronounce. It is my honest opinion that a large percentage of men today have never experienced true, Biblical salvation. They may have made a commitment. They may have prayed a prayer. They may go to church and read their Bible occasionally and pray, but there is something missing. They are miserable. They are restless. They are bombarded with depression, temptations and lustful thoughts. They are searching for something and don't even know where to start. The problem is simple. They have never been regenerated. They have never been born again. They are religious, but lost. That is the reason that I have dedicated my life to preaching the simple gospel of Jesus Christ. I have personally experienced the saving power of the gospel, and I have seen it work in lives. I've seen drunkards and dope addicts transformed by the simple message of the gospel. I have also seen preachers, deacons and church members acknowledge that they had never been saved and submit their lives to the saving power of Jesus. My friend, it works.

Trying to live the Christian life apart from Christ is not only exhausting, it is downright impossible. Knowing the routines and playing the game will only increase your frustration. In my years in the ministry, I have met many men that came to me for counseling. Every problem you can imagine has been brought for me to "fix." They would come to me, usually as a last resort, to help them with their crisis. Men that had been unfaithful to their wives and didn't know how to handle it. Men suffering from depression. Men that were battling thoughts of suicide. Men that were frustrated because they couldn't get motivated to do more for God than what they were already doing, which was nothing. Men that were battling sexual lusts and immoral desires. After talking with these men, I found out that most of them had one common problem – they had never been born again.

In John chapter three, Jesus was confronted one night by a man as religious as the day is long. His name was Nicodemus, and the Bible says he was a ruler of the Jews. He was looked up to by all the people as a man of God; a man that knew the law like the back of his hand. No doubt he was a moral man. I am sure he was responsible, mature, hardworking, sober and respected for his intelligence. As the story unfolds, something very peculiar is revealed about this man. He had no idea what it meant to be born again. In fact, in his efforts to try to understand the concept of being born again, he made one of the most ignorant statements found in the Bible. Jesus told him, "…Verily, verily, I say unto thee, Except a man be born again, he cannot see the kingdom of God." Nicodemus responded with this absurd question. "How can a man be born when he is old?

can he enter the second time into his mother's womb, and be born?" Here was a man of extraordinary intelligence, religious knowledge and influence making a complete fool of himself! He had no idea what Jesus was talking about.

The Proofs of Salvation

The problem that I have seen among men is that many of them cannot grasp the fact that not only does the Bible give the plan of salvation, but it also gives proofs of it. It is very easy to determine if you have ever been truly saved or not. You do not have to guess. You do not have to ask somebody else. God's word will reveal to you if you have been saved or not because there will be evidence of salvation. Until you have perfect peace that you have been supernaturally regenerated, you can forget being an exceptional man in God's eyes.
God's word gives an undeniable proof of salvation in II Corinthians 5:17. He said, "Therefore if any man be in Christ, he is a new creature: old things are passed away; behold, all things are become new." This verse takes away all the guess work. The facts are quite plain: if there has never been a supernatural change in your life, then you have never been saved! It is not praying a prayer. It is not being baptized. It is not being confirmed. It is not being born into a Christian home or having good morals or being a nice guy. Salvation is a divine work of God in your heart that brings about a definite, immediate and continual change! Notice some of the definite changes that being born again will bring about in a man's life.

- Forgiveness of sins - "In whom we have redemption through his blood, even the forgiveness of sins:" (Colossians 1:14).
- Peace like never before - "Therefore being justified by faith, we have peace with God through our Lord Jesus Christ:" (Romans 5:1).

- A hunger for the Word of God – "As newborn babes, desire the sincere milk of the word, that ye may grow thereby:" (I Peter 2:2).
- A genuine love for the people of God – "We know that we have passed from death unto life, because we love the brethren. He that loveth not his brother abideth in death" (I John 3:14).
- Power to overcome temptation – "Ye are of God, little children, and have overcome them: because greater is he that is in you, than he that is in the world" (I John 4:4).
- Boldness to tell people what Christ did for you - "For the scripture saith, Whosoever believeth on him shall not be ashamed" (Romans 10:11).
- A serious desire to obey God's word – "And hereby we do know that we know him, if we keep his commandments" (I John 2:3).
- Rejection of worldly things – "Love not the world, neither the things that are in the world. If any man love the world, the love of the Father is not in him" (I John 2:15).
- A real relationship with Jesus Christ – "If we say that we have fellowship with him, and walk in darkness, we lie, and do not the truth:" (I John 1:6).
- A clear conscience – "Holding the mystery of the faith in a pure conscience" (I Timothy 3:9).
- An attitude of joy – "Yet I will rejoice in the LORD, I will joy in the God of my salvation." (Habakkuk 3:18).
- Listening to the Holy Spirit – "And grieve not the holy Spirit of God, whereby ye are sealed unto the day of redemption" (Ephesians 4:30).

There are many, many more evidences of a person that has been truly saved by the grace of God. If the changes listed above have not occurred in your life, you are in trouble! When God saves a person, He changes them. He performs a divine "heart transplant" and when He does it, He does it right. The results are people with a changed heart, a changed life and a changed purpose. The evidence of true salvation is a changed person. Have you been changed?

There are so many men today that are faking Christianity. If they could be perfectly honest, they would admit that they have no desire for church, God, the Bible or anything spiritual. Many men just go along to appease their wives. They play along to keep peace in the home. Some do not even understand that there is more to Christianity than empty professions and rituals. They do not realize that what they have is hollow and absolutely useless. They grew up in church, and it is just a part of life. It is respectable, and it makes them look like decent citizens, so they play along. They'd much rather be playing golf or sitting at home watching TV. They make their kids go only because they had to go when they were a kid. There are really many reasons why men play the church game, but the final score will be the same for every one that does.

Where Are You Going When You Die?

God's word, the Final Authority for all matters of faith and practice, gives the final outcome of that game way in advance. "And whosoever was not found written in the book of life was cast into the lake of fire." (Revelation 20:15). What about all those that went to church and was involved in the ministry? Are they guaranteed Heaven? Not hardly! Salvation is not good works. Salvation is not a verbal profession of faith in God. Salvation is an inward regenerating work of God that comes about only after a man has repented of his sins and is ready to make Jesus Christ the Lord of his life. The exceptional man's gospel is a gospel that brings about true change.

Being saved is not difficult. I heard the gospel message as a four-year-old boy and realized that I was lost and in need of salvation. I knelt at an old fashion altar and accepted Jesus Christ as my personal Savior. I asked Him to forgive me of all of my sins and birth me into His family. He did. Right then and there I became a child of God. Salvation is not difficult if you come with child-like faith. The difficult part is forsaking your pride and your mask of religion. What is difficult is coming to grips with the fact that you have been faking Christianity. The most difficult part of salvation is getting a man to acknowledge that he has never been saved and that he needs to. Until you can do that, you will never experience God's changing power in your life. You can forget having Him to help you and answer your prayers. You can forget ever being a man after God's own heart. You will never get saved until you get lost! Admitting that is the hardest part.

The only thing about you and me that God appreciates is what is done through the power of His Son, Jesus Christ. "But we are all as an unclean thing, and all our righteousnesses are as filthy rags;" (Isaiah 64:6). God is not impressed with your good deeds and good intentions. When He looks at you, all He is looking for is to see if the blood of Jesus Christ has been applied to your soul. If it has, He is pleased. If it hasn't, you stand condemned before a righteous and a holy God. "There is therefore now no condemnation to them which are in Christ Jesus, who walk not after the flesh, but after the Spirit" (Romans 8:1). The only way to experience true change in your life and to escape the condemnation of Almighty God is to kneel and ask for His free gift of salvation.

God is not interested in your works. He has already done everything that needs to be done to purchase your salvation. All you have to do is accept it. The substitutionary death of Jesus Christ paid your sin debt. In order to be saved, this is what you need to do. You must first admit that you are a sinner. God hates self-righteous pride. Until you admit that you need a Savior, then you cannot be saved! The first step to becoming a child of God is realizing that you are not already a child of God. Many people believe the false doctrine that we are all God's children. My friend, that is a lie of Satan. Everybody is not a child of God. If they are, then Jesus would not have said what He did in John 8:44, "Ye are of your father the devil, and the lusts of your father ye will do."

Those that are not saved, those that have never been born again, are a child of the devil. He controls them, he abuses them, he causes them to sin, he has them in chains and in bondage. But when you become a child of God, all of that changes. "But as many as received him, to them gave he power to become the sons of God, even to them that believe on his name:" (John 1:12).

Admitting that you are a sinner is the most difficult step of salvation for many people. They have lied to themselves and convinced themselves that they are OK. They think that when they die their good works will be weighed against their bad works and whichever way the scales are leaning will determine where they will go. That is not what God said. Even good, moral people will be condemned to Hell. "Many will say to me in that day, Lord, Lord, have we not prophesied in thy name? and in thy name have cast out devils? and in thy name done many wonderful works? And then will I profess unto them, I never knew you: depart from me, ye that work iniquity" (Matthew 7:22, 23). These verses have to be, without a doubt, the most horrifying words to ever fall on human ears. Image being a priest, pastor, church worker, even a person that performed miracles and cast out devils, and not be saved! Think about standing before an Almighty God and hearing Him say, "I never knew you!" How tragic! Just because you are a good person does not mean that you are going to Heaven. It is a serious mistake to think that!

Believing Jesus is the Only Way

If you have other plans or methods of getting to Heaven, you will never get there. Jesus said in John 14:6, "I am the way, the truth and the life: no man cometh unto the Father but by me." The Bible is very clear - you must believe that Jesus is the only way for salvation. If you are depending on good works, baptism, confirmation, church membership, giving money to the church or whatever, you are not saved!

God is not interested in your good works when it comes to getting saved. He is only interested in your TRUST and FAITH in the finished work that Christ did on the cross. Until you can place all your trust in what Jesus did for you at Calvary, then your good works are worthless. Look at what the Bible says in Romans 10:9, "That if thou shalt confess with thy mouth the Lord Jesus, and shalt believe in thine heart that God hath raised him from the dead, thou shalt be saved." It is very clear on the fact that our salvation comes not through works, but by the mercy and grace of God.

Ephesians 2:8 and 9 says, "For by grace are ye saved through faith, and that not of yourselves, it is the gift of God. Not of works lest any man should boast." Salvation is a gift! Did you know that it is called a "gift" dozens of times in the Word of God? Do you earn a gift? Do you purchase a gift? Do you work for a gift? Of course not! A gift is given to you by someone who loves you. If you had to work for it, it would not be a gift. It would be wages, wouldn't it? Well, the Bible already told us that the wages that we deserved was death! So, God has given us what we did not deserve. That is called grace. The grace of God is God's unearned favors though we do not deserve them. If you try to get to Heaven any other way than by complete trust in His free gift of salvation, then you will never make it. To try and earn God's gift is the ultimate insult to Him.

Repent of Your Sins

Repentance simply means a change of heart, a change of mind and a change of will. If you are sick and tired of your sinful heart and sinful ways, then God wants to save you today. Jesus preached, "Except ye repent, ye shall all likewise perish." If you love your sin so much that you are not interested in repentance, then you can't get saved! You have to be willing to leave your sinful life and become a new creature in Christ Jesus! If you are not willing to repent, God will see that you are not sorry for your sins and will not save you. Salvation is not based on your works, but God is looking at your heart to see if you are serious about being saved.
I John 1:9 says, "If we confess our sins, he is faithful and just to forgive us our sins, and to cleanse us from all unrighteousness." Being honest about your sins and getting forgiveness for them is very important. Until you do that, you can't be saved. It is my prayer that by reading this gospel message, the Holy Spirit of God has convinced you that you are a sinner and in need of salvation. Christ is the only way. He was born of a virgin, lived a sinless, perfect life, was crucified for your sins, and was buried. Three days later He rose from the grave. He is alive today, sitting at the right hand of God. He wants to give you the gift of everlasting life and to forgive you of all your sins. Don't wait. Don't procrastinate. Don't doubt Him or His love for you. Trust and accept Him before it is too late.

You are not promised another day. There is no guarantee that you'll live to be an old man. You could die today. Your house is on fire. Get out and run to Jesus. He will save you from that awful place called Hell and you will never regret it. The question still remains - "Where are you going when you die?" If you cannot remember a time and place when you were born again, then you need to be saved today. To wait would be the height of foolishness.

You have just read the most important message ever given. It is a message of salvation, love and hope. If you realize that you have never been saved, why don't you do so now? Why don't you get on your knees right now and humbly admit to God that you are a sinner and that you need to be saved. Ask Him to come into your life and make you a child of God. Let Him know that you are not trusting in your works, but instead you are trusting in the death, burial, and resurrection of Jesus for your salvation. Repent of your sins and ask Him to save you, and He will. Don't put it off. Ask Him today! If you do accept Jesus as your personal Savior, I'd love to hear about it. Please contact me and let me know so that I can rejoice with you.

Pastor M. S. Shiflett
pastorss@pleasantview.org

For a complete list of books by author M. S. Shiflett, visit the Pleasant View Baptist Publications website.
www.pleasantview.org